Outline Guide
to
Pottery

Outline Guide
to
Pottery

Tony Birks

With drawings by Michael Woods

Blandford Press

Acknowledgment

From the conception of this book to its completion, I have had the benefit of the invaluable help and advice of Michael Woods, Director of Art at Charterhouse.

This book was designed and produced by Alphabet and Image, Sherborne, Dorset.

First published by Blandford Press Ltd 1975

Filmset by Specialised Offset Services Ltd, Liverpool
Printed in Great Britain by Redwood Burn Ltd, Trowbridge & Esher

ISBN: 0 7137 0738 0

Contents

1 A Circle of Magic

Enter an active potter's workshop, anywhere, and you are likely to fall under the spell of pottery. It may only be a brief enchantment – an experience which contrasts with familiar details in a highly specialized world – but you will be looking in upon an activity which has been going on for thousands of years, a method, material and a product which never changes. Whether the potter's workshop is in a city basement or in a peaceful village, anywhere in the world, certain features will be common to all. Provided it is a small establishment, you will see work in all stages of production, damp 'ware' fresh from the wheel or hand, a cluster of clay-covered tools surrounding the centre of operations, whether it be the wheel or the workbench, and clay dust on the floor and shelves. Of course, making pottery for a living is hard work – hard physical work – an exhausting strain if the potter is determined to maintain and improve high artistic standards, and few potters are rich men. Yet the visitor to the pottery often envies the potter his way of life, his contact with his material, his achievement single-handed of a finished product; the making of something from nothing, or rather the creation of an object from meaningless uniform matter.

The autonomy of the full-time potter's life is hedged about with problems of marketing, raw materials rising in price, and the inevitability of many factory-made articles being more accurately produced and cheaper than his own. But you, his visitor, envy him his freedom, his link with the past, his reliance on the present, and most of all, his skill in causing to rise from the wheel in seconds a cylinder, a bowl, a vase, a jar. Few people can resist this magical experience.

Luckily pottery is one of the crafts best provided for by evening classes in adult education centres, and can easily be practised at home. The only vital equipment is a kiln, more basic than the wheel. It is by means of a kiln – by putting a clay shape into a high temperature – that pottery is made, a material that is strong and will not, like clay, disintegrate in water.

The process of pot-making is as follows. The drying of a piece of pottery after shaping removes all the 'free' water. The chemically combined water in the clay is freed when the temperature reaches about 500°C. Above 650°C the material becomes hardened and ceases to be softenable, though it is technically known as 'soft'. Around 1000°C, all organic materials have burned away and the pot has become really hard, though still porous. At around this temperature the pottery is usually cooled, and taken from the kiln. It is now called a 'biscuit' pot. It has the porosity and often also the colour of an earthenware plant pot. The pot is next coated with a material which will melt into glass when it is returned to the kiln for a second 'firing'. According to its constituents, the glass or 'glaze' melts at temperatures ranging from 850°C to 1300°C, and it is, of course, fluid when the melting point is reached. It is not left long at this temperature, or taken higher, as this would cause the liquid glass to run off altogether. Thus temperatures and glazes are carefully related. The many glazes which melt between 1000°C and 1100°C are called earthenware glazes. Those which melt between 1250°C and 1300°C are called stoneware. Above 1200°C clay itself becomes dense like stone, and it is no longer porous. Its heavy body material makes it proof against sudden shocks of temperature such as being popped into a hot domestic oven, and so stoneware is sometimes called ovenware.

Not all clays are suitable for making stoneware – they explode or crack at high temperatures – and not all kilns will reach such

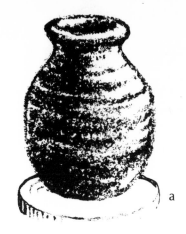

a

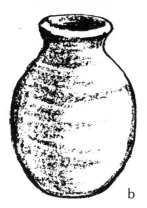
b

c

d

e

*The freshly made pot **a** will shrink a little as it dries (**b**). It must be bone dry before it is 'fired'. When it comes out of the kiln it will have shrunk again and is now a porous and insoluble 'biscuit' pot, as shown in **c**. Glaze and decoration are applied to the surface (**d**), and after another firing the pot is complete (**e**).*

high temperatures, so most of the pots you are likely to make as a beginner will be fired with earthenware glazes in a low-temperature kiln.

The drama of kilns and firing them fills many books, and indeed it is worthy of them. From a sawdust kiln in a biscuit tin to a multi-chambered Japanese rising kiln or an open bonfire kiln in Africa, the subject is full of excitement and it is tempting to devote more space than one ought in an outline guide to pottery to the different ways of bringing a pot up to temperature. For those who want to build their own kilns a list of useful references is given on page 98. For those who hope to get along without one, one must sadly restate that there is no way of making real pottery without a furnace at least three times as hot as a domestic oven.

The energy source, which can be wood, coal, electricity, gas or oil, affects the design and the cost of the kiln. But in essence a kiln is simply a chamber surrounded by material that will stand high temperatures and provide insulation from the surroundings. Sometimes the pots inside the chamber are exposed to direct heat from flames – sometimes they are muffled from it by a dividing wall of bricks. An electric kiln is much like a battery of electric radiators aimed towards one another in an enclosed space. Most earthenware is produced in electric kilns, which are the least expensive to buy and the most likely to be installed at an evening institute.

If the key to pottery is the kiln, then the substance of course is the clay. Its character is described in the next chapter, and many readers will already be impatient for practical instruction and an end to definition. However, I cannot justify a plunge into yet another instructional book on pottery without stating its aim simply and clearly. I am saddened by the attitude that a potter must, with reverence for an ancient, noble craft, accept failure and tolerate low standards of finish for his pots which he would not accept in a home-made curtain or a picture frame. Bad pots abound because techniques are misapplied and standards of judgment are confused. Indeed a 'bad pot' is not as easy to define as, say, a badly made bookshelf. In the instructions, diagrams and drawings which follow, however, I have tried to follow the principle that techniques, forms, materials and decoration should be compatible, and that the end product should not be beyond the complete beginner. A wobbly first attempt on the wheel or made with coils of clay becomes horribly permanent when fired. This book is written on the basis that it is better to produce a simple clean result that is useful and satisfying than to struggle with an ambitious project that does not work.

A pot that looks as though it was made in a kindergarten may have taken a long time to make and may have taught the maker something about the handling of clay, but it brings little joy. Beginners are bound to make mistakes, but if they match a technique with a clear idea of what they want there is no reason why they should not be pleased with the finished pot.

2 Clay

Gardeners, on the whole, are not fond of clay. It is frustrating and obtuse at the end of a spade, and can be remarkably, infuriatingly, pure. It is the same stuff that pots are made of. It is sticky, heavy and fine-grained. Garden clay as found all over the world, often yellow or slate grey in colour, *can* be used for your pots, but the slightest trace of soil or root will ruin it, affect its plasticity and spoils its chances of survival in the kiln. To dig the drainage system for my present pottery, a deep trench had to be made through fine yellow clay. A century ago this material would have been used, not wasted, but the immense effort involved in separating and sieving out the fine particles, and then drying the clay, does not makes sense, since prepared clay bought by the bagful is cheap. Thus my trench was filled in with much the same material that I was going to use in the workshop, and which I buy ready prepared. Most craft shops sell it, and it is cheaper in large quantities. It is usually available in 'red' or 'white', more accurately described by colour as chocolate-brown or grey. If you are buying it for yourself, I would recommend you to choose white, since this gives you more opportunity for decoration of the pottery you make at a later stage, although at an evening class you may have no choice. Red is more common, for it is less pure and it is a little cheaper. It is very suitable for all hand-made pots and also for work on the wheel, so do not be discouraged if there is nothing else. Craft shops sell materials called 'cold clay' or 'duo clay', which hardens and can be used for things like ashtrays without the need for firing in a kiln. I cannot recommend it for I have never tried it, neither can I dismiss it as a useful material for the kiln-less, but I understand that it cannot be fired in a kiln without disintegrating.

Preparing the clay

The best companion for a piece of pottery clay is a sheet of polythene. The one wrapped round the other will keep the clay indefinitely from drying into a hard, non-plastic lump, and it is vital to make sure that any clay wrapped up in polythene for long-time storage is securely wrapped so that no air can get in. It is not that clay 'goes off' like cheese, for it simply needs softening with water if it is too hard in order for it to be reconditioned, but all this takes time and it is very irritating for a beginner who wants to get on with the job.

It is easy to decribe how to keep clay in good condition, but much harder to describe in words the exact 'feel' of plastic clay this is right for working, whether for hand building or working on the wheel. An experienced potter can tell by the pressure of a thumb against the clay if it is too wet or too dry for the particular technique he is going to use. If it is too wet he will spread it out on an absorbent surface such as a plaster of Paris slab or a piece of clean, unpainted wood. If it is slightly too dry he will make finger holes in the lump (see drawing), fill these with water and remould the clay so that the water is quickly dispersed through the lump. If you have no teacher to guide you and are not sure if the pottery clay you have bought is in the right state for working you can test it as follows. Take a piece the size of a small carrot, and roll it under your dry hand on a very smooth surface like a formica-topped table. Roll it into a long sausage – a technique you will need to learn later in order to make coil pots – and if it sticks to your hand or the table it is too wet. If it is too dry, fine cracks will appear running either across the roll or along its length. If you pick up the roll and it will hang limply over your finger like a

Finger holes made in clay which is too dry to work, filled with water, will help the clay to soften up so that it can be kneaded within a few minutes.

worm without breaking, it is in fine condition, though you will have to check that the body of clay you are going to use has the same consistency throughout and no air holes or foreign matter.

The beginner, keen to start on his pot, will again be disappointed to find that he will be asked at this stage to join in a ritual process of kneading the clay known as 'wedging'. I am not so sure that it actually does the clay any good to be spiralled around as shown in the diagram in preparation for being made into a pot, if it is shown to be already smooth and even throughout when cut across at regular intervals with a wire or nylon thread, but I am quite sure that many beginners make its condition worse by rolling it about or pushing at it so that it sticks to the workbench and to their hands. If your clay *is* uneven it needs wedging, and it is essential to grasp the necessary movement within the clay. It must circulate. As the heel of your hand presses down on the clay, the fingertips turn up the far edge of the lump, ready for the next downward pressure. The diagrams

*You cannot knead clay simply by pressing on it with the heel of the hands. You have to raise the clay at the far edge of the lump with the fingertips before pressing down so that the clay in the lump will circulate. The diagram **above** shows the clay being kneaded into a spiral by turning the lump each time it is raised. Beginners may find it easier to knead the clay straight, as shown **right**.*

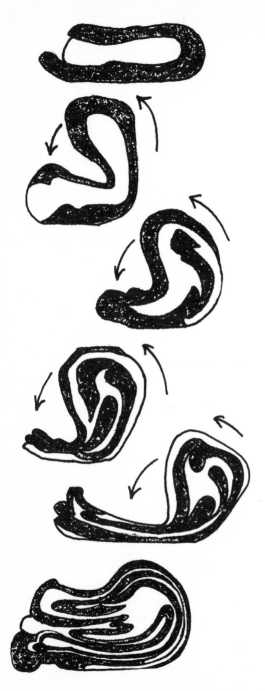

left show what happens in cross-section. Getting the knack of wedging is usually only a matter of a few minutes, and once acquired it will not be lost. It is a question of rhythm and co-ordination. Learn it, or get someone to prepare your clay for you. It is sadly true that pots made from uneven, lumpy or aerated clay will probably be failures.

Remember to prepare enough clay for all the pots you intend to make in one session, whether an evening class or an evening at home, and if you fail to complete a pot in one evening keep both the clay and unfinished work carefully wrapped up with polythene so that when you finish the job later you are using the same material as that with which you started. You can add things to it, to change its colour or its texture, and you may, when it is turned into a pot, paint or pour other materials over its surface for decorative purposes or purely functional ones – to make it watertight. These techniques are described in later chapters, but in the next chapter we will deal with tools – the aids the potter uses in addition to his own fingers for pot-making.

The tools reflect the two outstanding characteristics of clay from the artist's point of view. First, it can be shaped by hand or around something, and will keep its shape. Secondly, it can take an impression, and keep that too. Just as dogs' pawprints are immortalized in fresh concrete, so dinosaurs' footprints are kept by clay, in this instance for hundreds of millions of years, and in remarkable detail.

Press your thumb into a ball of prepared clay. Your fingerprint will be taken as accurately as in any police record. This ability to keep impressions adds a dimension to the creative potential of clay and to its usefulness.

To show what happens inside a lump of clay during the kneading process, clays of contrasting colours were folded together. After five of the rotating movements of kneading the clays are becoming mixed, as can be seen in the cross-sections **left**. *You must continue to knead the clay until the texture is absolutely even when you slice it across with the nylon thread shown* **right**.

3   Tools and Tiles

An array of tools from jolley arms to asbestos gloves is displayed in the catalogues of the ceramic suppliers listed on page 98. It is as well to have one of these catalogues as a handy reference, but do not be dismayed by the range of tools available. Most of them have domestic equivalents – kitchen knives, scales, skewers, polythene jugs and sponges.

Some containers are useful: plastic bowls and jugs for keeping and handling liquids, rigid transparent plastic biscuit boxes for storing unfinished work. The rest of the hand tools fall into the category of shapers, cutters, markers and guides. For cutting clay you will need a sharp pointed knife and at least two 'turning' tools, as illustrated. They can be home-made, but they must be of heavy-gauge metal. You will also need a steel ruler, preferably marked with centimetres or inches, a plastic or wooden set square, and a good length of nylon fishing trace or steel wire. This, with a toggle of wood at each end, has a multitude of uses including acting like a cheese wire, so that the inside of a lump of prepared clay can be examined for faults.

Amongst the shapers, you will need sandpaper, a 'rubber kidney', more easily bought than made and invaluable for use with the press moulds described in Chapter 5, a wooden modelling tool with a flattened end like a fingernail, and an old hacksaw blade which is flexible and serrated for use on hand-built pottery. Finally, you will need a rolling pin and two working surfaces, one of which

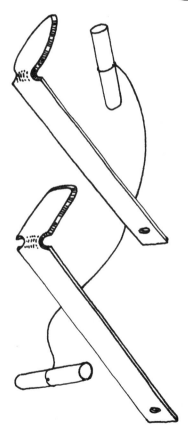

Two turning tools and a nylon thread cutter.

is absorbent, like a wooden bench, and another which is non-absorbent, such as a marble slab.

Other tools are used in the decoration of clay, for example, paintbrushes, seals and stamps. A clay surface, whether it is the flat surface of a tile or the curved surface of a bottle, can be decorated while the clay is still damp. A design can be cut right through it with a knife (or a quill-shaped metal tool for circular holes) leaving a filigree of clay. Designs can be impressed into it either singly with a stamp or in a repeating pattern with a roller in much the same way as a bicycle tyre leaves tracks in the mud.

A clay surface can also be built up into relief by the addition of clay in strips or wads, or patterns cast from moulds – an ancient and popular technique known as 'sprigging'.

The making of pots begins in the next chapter, but whilst we are concerned with basics, the rest of this chapter gives instruction and hints on the making of a very basic ceramic – the tile.

Tiles

Just as the fabric of the houses that many of us live in is made of clay fired into bricks, so the walls with which we are surrounded are often covered with fired and decorated clay. Tiles are often also used and decorated singly; they are sometimes framed in groups like paintings or made into trays, or, with a layer of cork underneath they are used as individual insulators or table mats. This is a long step from the floor or wall covering for which they were intended. On floors or walls, tiles must be smooth so that they can be washed and do not collect dirt. Many buildings like hospitals use tiles inside; others, like pubs and shops, have them outside, where they are often used to attract the eye with a bold pattern or colour – such as nail-head or Greek key design – which is dazzling as a mass. Often a pattern can be created which is larger than the tile unit simply by varying the position of the decorated tiles, as on many Central American and South European house facades. The unit, however, remains the key, and this is small – often 15 centimentres (6 inches) square – because

*All four tiles shown **right** are the same, but their arrangement gives a pattern unit which is larger than the individual tile. A pattern like this, in several colours on a white ground, can be made by using a paper stencil – see Chapter 9.*

Clay for tiles must have an even thickness; the wooden guides on each side of the clay ensure this.

when clay is thin it is inclined to warp under the effect of drying and heat. It presents tile manufacturers with a nice problem of control and prevents the widespread use and manufacture of large tiles.

The beginner or home potter can make tiles easily and quickly provided he does not try to make them too large or too thin. A 10 centimetre (4 inch) unit is as large a size as the home potter should aim for. The thickness of the clay you use is important: 6 millimetres is a minimum and this thickness must be constant. You achieve this by placing two pieces of wood of equal thickness one on each side of a lump of clay within the span of the rolling pin, as shown in the diagram, and rolling the clay on top of a piece of fabric or stiff paper on a flat surface. The wooden guides will govern entirely the thickness, or rather the thinness, to which you can roll the clay. They should be carefully matched and about 30 centimetres long so that you can make quite a large slab of clay. These two pieces of wood are invaluable for several of the pot-making techniques described in this book.

Make sure that the clay you use is dry enough not to stick to the rolling pin. Sprinkling a little powdered clay evenly over the lump will help to dry it and stop the surface 'plucking'. The clay you use must be prepared as described in Chapter 2, but it is a good idea to let it harden a little before working. Remember that the stiffer the clay you can roll out into a slab the crisper will be the tile.

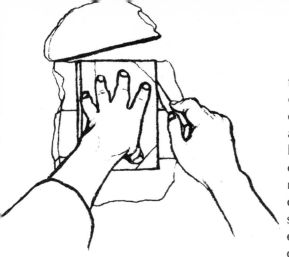

Make sure your tiles are square and the cut you make is vertical.

Simple tile cutters in a size 10 centimetres square can be bought from ceramic suppliers. These are much like spring-loaded pastry cutters and are pressed down into the slab of clay. Without such a cutter you can make a set of tiles using a ruler and a set square or any right-angled shape like a book, and cutting them with a sharp knife. Cutting the tiles is not particularly hazardous. Make parallel cuts exactly 10 centimetres (4 inches) apart and then, using your right-angled guide, cut across, making the cuts slowly so that the corners of the tiles are not pulled out of shape. The tiles should be separated slightly, taking care not to finger-mark the surface. The edges can be softened or cushioned if you wish by pressing them down very gently with the flat of the ruler. The tiles should be allowed to dry slowly for a day, and then turned over to avoid the slight curling up of the corners which happens when the top side dries more quickly than the base. Keep turning the tiles regularly. If you make them at an evening class, take them home with you in a box so that you can supervise their drying.

Undecorated small tiles – say 5 centimetres across – glazed alternately in dark and light colours can make an excellent chess board if cemented and grouted on to a base, or a checkerboard panel to hang on a wall. Alternate plain glazing gives tremendous opportunity for varied patterns, using the tile as the pattern unit.

If you want to make a decorative wall panel from tiles you can incise a design with a comb or a pencil point all over the slab before cutting the tiles. Otherwise, incised patterns can be made on the individual tiles, the hollows later taking up the glaze attractively when the ceramic is complete.

If you add pieces of clay to the surface of the tile, as shown on the next page, make sure that they are clearly defined shapes and firmly fixed on. Rings thrown on the wheel (see Chapter 8) can be added and these can be 'luted' on to the surface of a not-too-dry tile by scoring the correct place on the tile with a pin, wetting the score marks with water or 'slip' (a mixture of clay and water with the consistency of thin cream), and pressing the addition into place. You will find a modelling tool useful for tidying up such raised tiles. Tiles decorated with projecting forms are good at gathering dust, and can only be used as wall panels as their surface is too uneven for a table top. Any panel of tiles, however, is well within the capabilities of the beginner, and is a good project for someone who wants to see a happy outcome to their first confrontation with clay.

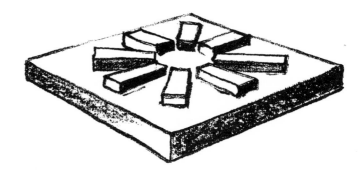

Some simple raised designs on tiles, which can be used to make decorative wall panels. Aim to keep the forms crisp and avoid handling before the tiles are completely dry.

4 Small Pots and Jewellery

Small pots do not necessarily come before large pots. A beginner who wants to tackle a large rugged pot should turn straight to Chapter 7; he may want to try his hand at more delicate ones later. Those who want to make small ceramic objects must be prepared to make them very carefully, and one method is 'pinching'.

Pinched bowl

By taking a small ball of prepared clay – small enough to lie in the palm of your hand – you can pinch this into the shape of a hollow ball by using the thumb of the right hand to make the hollow while rotating the ball in the palm of the other hand. As the hollow becomes larger, so will the pot, the walls will become thinner and the ball will soon be the size and shape of a small scooped-out half-grapefruit. By curving the fingers of the left hand which holds the bowl, you can prevent the diameter from becoming too wide, and by pleating the clay near the rim you can obtain a more pleasing spherical shape. Precision is not an appropriate word to use with regard to pinched shapes, for they never rival wheel-made or moulded pots for symmetry, but they can be very pleasing if the shape is well controlled. If the clay is too dry it will crack near the rim, and the hands have a rapid drying effect on the surface. Moistening the right hand slightly may help, but the left hand which holds the bowl must be kept dry, or the whole pot will become sticky.

When the form is complete, the pot, held in both hands by its walls, should be tapped lightly on the table to flatten out a 'base', and this will give it essential stability if it is later to be glazed and used as a flower container.

It is likely that the surface you have made will be rather like beaten pewter, with small facets made by the fingers. Do not try to remove these. They are part and parcel of the technique. Well-finished does not mean smoothed off; it means stopping when the pot looks just right – this moment is not always easy to judge, as anyone involved in creative work knows. The precedent for making beautiful pots by pinching, however, is an ancient one – Japanese ceremonial tea bowls have been made in this way for many centuries and they still are.

Jewellery

Like pinched pottery, ceramic jewellery can be made in a small space at home. Fired clay has many of the characteristics of stone, and ceramic jewellery is rather like jewellery made from pebbles, except that the potter has control of the shape and is not dependent on what he finds on the beach. One thing he must learn from the pebble, however, is that anything which is worn next to the skin must have a rounded non-scratchy edge. Small clay pieces, whether they are to be glazed or not, must be softly curved at the edge and must be made of a smooth clay. Even if worn over wool, a sharp-edged ceramic will be unpopular.

Take a ball of clay the size of a horse chestnut and squeeze it tightly between the palms of your two hands. It will take up the form of a convex lens, perhaps with some of the lines from your palm crossing it as ridges. Because it has no sharp edges it will make an ideal pendant blank, and can be decorated by incising a simple pattern with a tool like a kitchen fork or impressing with a solid object like the knurled end of a lipstick case.

Unlike a pebble from the beach, there is no problem in making a hole in the pendant so that it can be strung on a leather thong. Press a sharp pencil point through the wad of clay while it is still

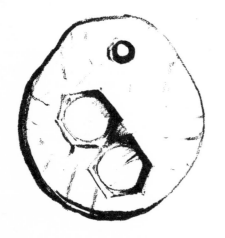

Clay pendant with impressed design.

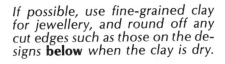

If possible, use fine-grained clay for jewellery, and round off any cut edges such as those on the designs **below** *when the clay is dry.*

plastic, making the same hole from both sides, again to avoid sharp edges.

Pendants of more controlled shape can be made by cutting rolled-out slabs of clay with a knife, and these can be perforated with an ease which the metal worker would envy. The drawings suggest how composite jewellery can be made by threading together beads and clay shapes, and the combinations are unlimited. Remember however that clay is heavy – as heavy as metal – so keep the units small and fairly thin.

Composite designs, like those shown **left**, *can be used for pendants or earrings.*

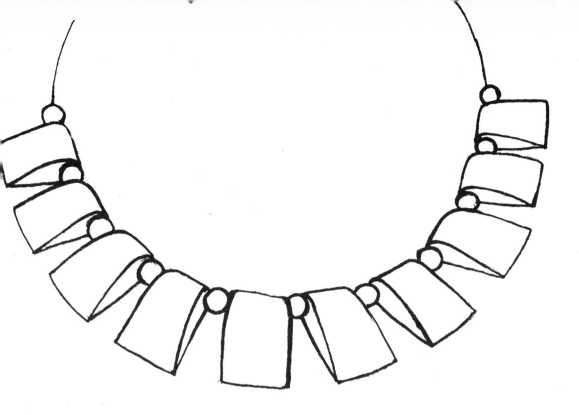

Necklace

Each of the units on the necklace can be decorated if desired with repeating or varying designs.

In order to make a necklace of the kind illustrated above you will need to roll out clay much thinner than for tiles – 4 millimetres is adequate. The cross-section need not be even. From a slab which thins to one edge, wedge shapes like tiny axe heads can be cut which when strung together, separated by clay or wooden beads, make a radiating pattern when the necklace takes up its inevitable curved shape on the wearer. Holes should be drilled with a pencil point or a needle through the sides of the units so that the pieces lie flat when they are strung.

Bracelets can be made in a similar way, but avoid projecting or hanging pieces since ceramic, though comfortable to wear, makes an ugly sound if its parts clink together or against something else like a side plate at a dining table.

25

Decoration

The decoration of clay is mainly described in Chapter 9, but for the jewellery-maker it is perhaps helpful to give some hints on decoration here. All-over colouring can be in the clay itself, which may be red clay or speckled by adding manganese dioxide powder (purple) or ochre (ginger). An all-over colour and a shiny surface can be made by glazing the pieces (see Chapter 10), and if you use an opaque white glaze, coloured designs can be painted on with a paintbrush, using metal oxides (see Chapter 9). A colouring oxide like copper oxide, obtainable from ceramic suppliers, can be sponged on to a pendant and then sponged off again before glazing, and any incised design will retain the colourant in its cracks which will fire to a bright turquoise-green in the kiln.

Undoubtedly, impressed designs are the most satisfactory for jewellery since nothing sticks out to scratch the skin or clothes, and the well created by the impressing tool happily contains any glaze, which may have an attractive quality like a precious stone if it is thick. Even scraps of broken glass placed in a hollow impressed shape will melt into a coloured pool when the piece is fired in the kiln, and keen jewellery makers can experiment with enamels and lustres.

Ceramic beads are difficult to glaze, but burnished smooth and left undecorated they can make a good foil to a shiny coloured shape in a composite design.

5 Moulded Pottery

It is extremely likely that the cups and saucers that you use, the dinner plates and teapot in your home, are made from moulds. Nearly all pottery is made commercially in this way, as it is the safest way of ensuring that you can repeat the same shape time and time again, and it is also very quick when you have a large number of moulds.

'Moulded' does not mean worked into shape as one might expect, it means cast from a mould, using the property of clay to take up the shape of whatever it is in close contact with. Dry clay cannot be used, of course. If the clay is plastic, it has to be pressed into the mould and forced against the master shape. If the clay is liquid, gravity will provide the necessary force, and the dampness in the clay will be absorbed by the walls of the mould – usually made of plaster of Paris. The use of very liquid clay, or 'clay slip', is universal in factories, but it has for the beginner problems of shrinkage when it dries, and its constituents have to be very carefully controlled. The amateur potter can make a 'slip' by mixing powdered or plastic clay and water and he will use it not only as a casting material for moulds but also as a cement (see Chapter 6) and as a medium of decoration (see Chapter 9). Clay and water slip, carefully sieved, can be used successfully in simple absorbent moulds by pouring the creamy liquid into the mould up to the top, leaving it there for about half an hour while the clay dries against the wall of the mould, and then pouring the

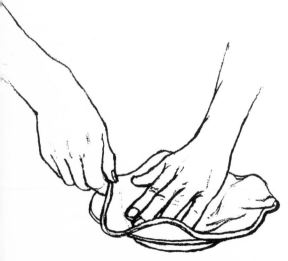

Clay behaves like pastry. With gentle pressure it can be made to follow the form of a shallow dish.

remaining slip out. The slip in the mould has to be topped up as liquid is lost into the mould wall, and great care has to be taken that the clay slip is competely even, by the sieving process using a fine mesh 'lawn', to avoid unevenness on the inside of the cast when the remaining liquid slip is poured off. Because of these hazards the beginner is advised to use plastic clay for moulded pottery. He will not, by this method, be able to make a complex pot like a teapot, but with a certain amount of invention, the use of moulds can be one of the most immediately satisfying ways of making a pot.

Two kinds of mould

When you have rolled out a slab of clay as for making tiles, you can either press it into a concave dish, as you might line a pie dish with pastry, or curve it over a convex shape, such as a darning mushroom or a car headlight lens. The important thing about the shape – whether convex or concave – is that it should not contain any sharp corners or undercut edges. The curves must be gentle ones. When clay is pressed on to or into the mould, the side which is in contact with the mould will reproduce the master shape exactly. The surface of the exposed side is up to you, and the degree of finish you can achieve with a finishing tool, or with fine sandpaper when the cast is dry. Take a large soup plate with a wide, flat rim and put a very light rubbing of grease such as lard on the inside. Feed your rolled-out slab of clay gently into the bowl, as if it were pastry. Persuade the clay with your fingers to follow the form, but do not press too hard on the clay or you will make permanent impressions with your fingertips. Cut round the edge of the clay with a sharp knife, keeping a steep and steady angle for the cut, and remove all the unwanted clay from the edge. A slightly dampened natural sponge can be used to smooth over the inside surface, though no tool is as good for this as the kidney-shaped piece of stiff rubber mentioned in Chapter 3 and sold by ceramic suppliers as a 'rubber kidney'. Such a tool is shown in the diagram, right, used with a bold sweep to avoid marking the clay.

When the clay lining to the soup plate has been carefully trimmed around the edge, the inside surface should be smoothed with a sponge or rubber kidney. Do this thoroughly and carefully – this is the surface you will see whenever you use the plate.

It is important to limit the amount of water you use – a couple of drops will lubricate the tool without softening the clay, which must not be allowed to become sticky.

The clay shrinks as it dries, and your soup plate will soon have made a cast of itself, slightly smaller than the original, and smaller again by the time it is fired.

Imagine using the same soup plate upside down, putting the rolled-out clay over the hump of its back. You can obtain a similar cast on this convex surface, but of course it will reproduce the details of the base – usually there is a slight foot ring which will appear as a hollow circle on the *inside* of your cast. There may also be some difficulty when the clay dries. It must not adhere to the plate or it will crack as it shrinks.

Some beginners are delighted to make a copy of existing pottery shapes in this way, as it provides them with a vehicle for their own decoration, either with slip or with painted colours as described in Chapters 9 and 10. It is not the only household vessel which can be used. Shallow pyrex dishes can produce ovenware casts, and the plastic or brass bowl of a pair of scales can make a deeper vessel, which can be given a foot for stability by adding a ring of clay to the convex centre of the hump before it dries.

However, a beginner who goes to an evening class laden with utensils of this kind is not likely to be popular, and he may well feel uninventive among his fellows, as he is not creating anything, only copying a ready-made shape. He will find it much more rewarding to make a mould to his own design, and his mould is likely to function better than a ready-made mould, for it will be made of absorbent material, either clay which has been fired in a kiln, or plaster of Paris.

The technique is ancient. The small pottery lamps which were used so widely in Classical times were made by making a solid master shape, firing it in the kiln, pressing the result into plastic clay so that the shape is 'taken', firing this in the kiln to make the mould or 'negative', and then pressing plastic clay into the negative mould to make the final hollow lamp. The beginner need not make anything so complicated as an oil lamp, and you

*Make a symmetrical pattern of the shape you want, using compasses for the corners, and draw a firm outline in ink on a cardboard base, as shown **below**. A stiff cardboard template **above** cut out to the profile of the mould can be used as a scraper.*

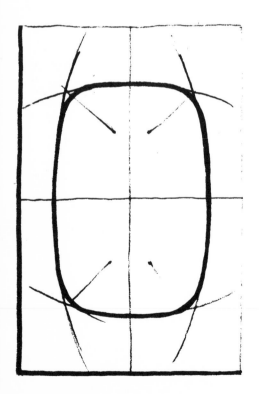

can cut down the three stages to two, but first you must make the master shape. I suggest you keep your subject fairly small – not more than 15 centimetres across. You should build up the form with solid clay. By using a thick cardboard template as shown in the diagram you can scrape the surface carefully to shape. Effort in making the shape symmetrical and without bumps is not wasted: the casts you make from moulds will reproduce every flaw in the original and you will be for ever irritated if you have decided to make do with a wobbly, unsure shape. Rulers and compasses are normally foreign to pottery made by hand, but beginners who build up the hump of clay on a cardboard pattern with the shape clearly drawn on, as shown in the diagram, have a helpful guide to stop them overstepping the mark.

When the master is complete it can be treated in two different ways. Firstly, it can be allowed to dry slowly, fired in the kiln and used as a hump mould. A thick, solid shape like this will break in the kiln unless it is bone dry before firing, or if the clay has not been prepared as described in Chapter 2. The hump mould will be much easier to use if you can attach to its underneath a robust stalk of clay like a mushroom stem before firing it. The three drawings on the next page show how a rolled-out piece of clay is draped over the hump mould, pressed to shape, and trimmed with a knife before it dries and hardens.

Secondly, your master can be used to make a plaster of Paris press-mould. With your master shape lying on a smooth surface build a wall of clay around the shape about 5 centimetres from the edge of the form and 2 centimetres higher than the form itself. Using surgical plaster (which can be bought in 7lb or 3 kg bags from chemists or drugstores) make a plaster mix by sprinkling the fine plaster into a polythene bowl containing about two litres of water. When the mixture is like thick cream and is completely freed from lumps by mixing with the hand, pour it over the clay form and up to the top of the surrounding wall. The plaster will harden and in about half an hour you can remove the wall and pull out the clay you have used as a master shape. The concave press-mould you have made can be used with sheets of plastic

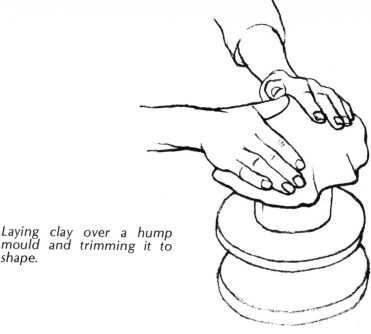

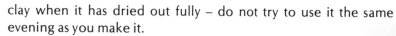

Laying clay over a hump mould and trimming it to shape.

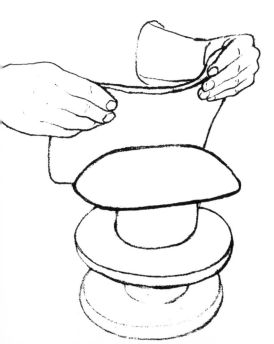

clay when it has dried out fully – do not try to use it the same evening as you make it.

Plaster of Paris is a material which does not go well with clay. Essential as it is in an active pottery, it is vital to keep bits of plaster out of the clay, and to avoid using clay for pot-making that has any fragments of plaster sticking to it. Clay with plaster in it will crack up in the kiln.

A Casserole

The practical shape for a casserole is oval or rectangular. It needs handles or lugs so that it can easily be taken out of the oven and it needs a lid which fits well and also has a handle big enough to grasp through an oven glove.

It is a daunting prospect for a beginner, though it is a very popular project, and if you use moulds you can make a very good casserole indeed. You must be sure to use stoneware clay if the result is to be ovenproof, and you should roll out with a rolling-pin sheets of clay not less than 5 millimetres thick. Using a press mould or a hump mould like the one illustrated on pages 30 and 31, make two identical casts. Prevent the first cast from drying out by covering it with polythene while you make the second one. The second cast will be the lid, and will need a flange adding to the inside of its rim as shown in the diagram. Score the inside edge of the rim with a knife or needle at the point marked **a** and add a little water or slip to this roughened surface. Then roll out a long strip of clay, cut it to an even width – perhaps 1.5 centimetres – with a ruler, and stick it all round the inside of the rim as shown in the cross-section, blending the two ends together where they meet. The flange you have made will have to be angled slightly inwards so that it fits snugly into the base, and you must try the two halves together to make sure they fit well. Avoid too much handling of the edges: your pot will look crude if they are uneven or dinted. Even leather-hard surfaces will stick to each other if left pressed together for a time, and you must avoid this by putting dry powdered clay or French chalk on the edges that will come into contact when you are testing the lid for its fit.

The diagrams show how the handles are added to the base and the lid. Make three sausages of clay by rolling the clay under your hands (see Chapter 7). Score small horizontal areas near the top of the sides of the casserole body, one at each end. Fill each roughened area with water or slip and press a sausage of clay against it. If the ends of the sausage are turned down and pressed by the fingers against the clay as shown in the diagram, a neat shape will result, and a handle or lug like this at each end will allow you to pick up the casserole easily. Do not try this, however, until the pot has been fired, for it will surely break.

The sausage used for the handle on the lid should be arched like a caterpillar or a cat's back to give a better grasp and insulation. It should be attached by pressing the ends on to scored areas on the long axis of the lid, as the drawing shows. Always make sure that there is a firm bond between handle and pot by using water and a scored surface to make a weld: there is a fuller description of this technique in Chapter 6 on slab pots. Do not press too hard when joining the handle to the form or you may

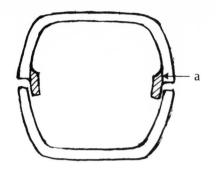

a

Cross-section of the casserole showing the flange attached to the lid.

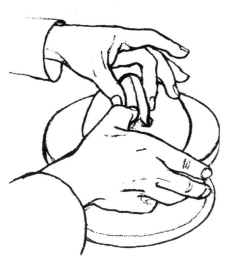

distort the shape, and try to keep the size of the handles in scale with the pot.

Allow your casserole to dry slowly, using a modelling tool to tidy up any rough parts, or by sandpapering when the pot is dry. The casserole should be fired if possible to a high temperature – over 1200°C – and if this is done it only needs glazing (see Chapter 10) on the inside.

Other shapes

A beginner who has managed successfully to make this fairly complicated form may feel confident about making other combined forms using moulds. Two identical casts can be joined together to make a flask shape, or a useful flower holder if the top side is perforated with holes at the leather-hard stage.

Those potters with an insatiable urge to make sets of pots should use moulds, for one of the advantages of the technique is that the moulds will deliver identical twins, triplets, or however many offspring you want. It is an easy way to make pots well, provided care is taken in designing the master shape.

*Do not press too hard when attaching the handles to your casserole (**above** and **left**), as it is easy to distort the shape when the clay is still damp.*

A flower holder with a perforated top made by joining two casts from a mould together at their rims. Make the holes in the top section before joining the two parts, or pieces of clay will rattle around in it for ever.

Slab construction by Bryan Newman.

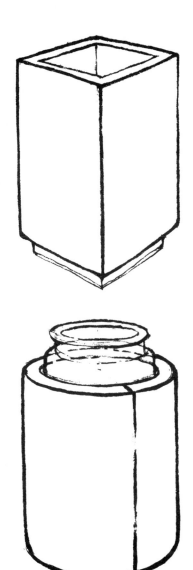

6 Slab Pottery

Pottery made out of slabs of clay can be of any size and of many kinds. Slab building requires the minimum of tools – only a knife, a straight edge and the same rolling pin and guide sticks as are used for tiles and press moulds.

Slabs of clay can be used as plane surfaces joined together at sharp angles to make a rather architectural form or else can be curved and bent, taking advantage of the generous compliance of damp clay, to make curved forms. These two extremes are illustrated alongside: the box, and the cylinder made by rolling a slab of clay around a jam jar. These examples are rather formal, however, and one of the attractions of slab pottery is its informality and the opportunity it gives for making unusual and sculptural shapes.

Technique

Taking a carefully wedged lump of clay, roll it to a flat slab between two height guides with the rolling pin, as illustrated on page 18. The natural tendency for the rolled-out clay is to stick to the bench, and the clay can be rolled on canvas or cotton cloth to keep it off the bench. The texture made by cloth, however, may not be what you want, and the clay slabs can be kept from sticking to the bench by putting a fine dusting of powdered clay or fine sand on the bench instead. The thickness of the slab should be governed by the size of the pot. There is no practical reason why different thicknesses of clay should not be used on a single pot, though it is not common to vary the thickness and the result is likely to be better balanced if they are even. A thickness of 6 millimetres is adequate for quite large pots, and if you are making slabs in any quantity it saves time to use an improvised cutter as illustrated in the drawing. Two pieces of wood, with notches every 6 millimetres cut in their sides, form the ends of the tool. A piece of nylon gut or wire is slotted into the lowest notch in each side and slices of clay of the correct thickness are made like the slices of a loaf of bread by pulling the wire through the lump of clay, and raising it by one notch on each side after each slice. The texture of the surface of slabs thus sliced will be quite different from that of clay rolled out like pastry: you must decide which texture you prefer and which best suits the pot you are to make.

When freshly made, a slab will have no great strength and will flop about if you try to stand it on edge. You must give it a chance to dry to a state like thick leather, but not to become so hard that, like a piece of cold toast, it breaks instead of bending between your fingers. If you want to sandwich the making of a slab pot within the two hours of an average evening class, you must prepare and roll out the slabs as soon as you arrive, and leave them on an absorbent surface to dry for about half an hour before turning them into a pot.

Shallow shapes can easily be made by moulds, as described in the previous chapter, and it is rather a waste to make out of slabs a shape which can be accurately press-moulded. I strongly advise you to have a clear idea in your mind of the shape you are going to make. It is not necessary to draw it first – indeed some first class potters are quite unable to draw – but drawings of the pot and plans of the sides can be very useful if they are cut out and used as templates for the slabs themselves. Slabs are not jointed together like carpentered wood. They are simply abutted together with water or a thin solution of slip used as 'glue'. The bond is made *much* stronger if the edges that will be in contact are scored with a knife or a pin as shown in the diagram. The water or slip applied

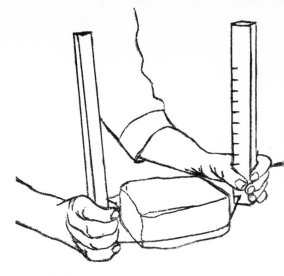

A home-made tool for cutting slabs of clay.

A modelling tool with a sharp point, a knife or a pin should be used to score grooves about 3 mm deep in the surfaces which are to be brought together.

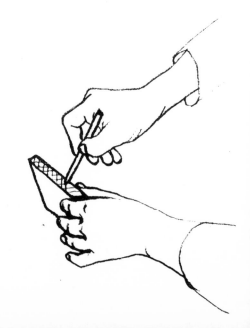

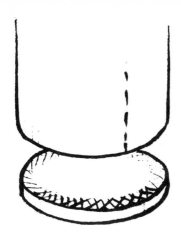

Joining a cylinder to its base.

A roller seal made from a carefully cut cork or piece of dowelling can be used to impress a continuous design on a clay slab.

with a brush or a sponge fills these cracks, softens the clay and makes a join not unlike that of welded metal.

The cylinder

To make the cylinder shown on page 35 you need a single piece of clay cut as a rectangle, another piece for the base and a former such as a jam jar around which the pot will be shaped. Score one edge of the rectangle as shown on p. 36, below, and having rolled the clay around a jar already dusted with French chalk to stop it sticking, cut away any surplus clay so that the two edges abut neatly. Squeeze a little water or thin slip into the join and press the edges firmly together. Your fingers will leave marks at the join which are quite attractive if they are regular, but the join can be hidden by adding a long, very thin 'worm' of clay along the join and smoothing it with a wooden modelling tool.

It is important now to take out the jar or whatever you have used as a former because clay shrinks as it dries and if it is left around the jar your pot will crack apart. The easiest way of adding the base is to stand the now hollow cylinder on a slab of clay and cut carefully round it with a knife; both the edge of the cylinder and the edge of the circular base should be scored as shown alongside, and slip added before the two surfaces are pressed finally together.

A cylindrical vase for flowers can thus be made without using a wheel and its standard of finish can be very high – a good deal depends on the rim at the top and how you choose to decorate the cylinder. If the rim is left flat with a sharp edge it will have the character of a slab pot rather than a pot which is trying to ape one made on the wheel, and the decoration on its sides can be impressed with seals or wheels (see diagram) *before* the side is cut out. This gives a special character when the plane surface is curved around which could not be achieved in a cylinder thrown on the potter's wheel.

The profile of a pot is very important indeed, and again and again it will be found that this profile is improved or clarified if it is

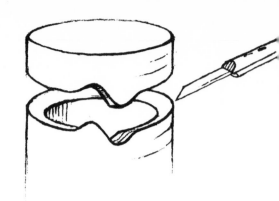

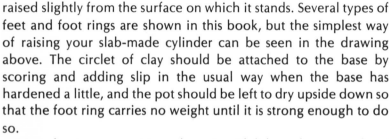

Attaching a foot ring to a cylinder **(left)**, *and making a notched lid* **(right)**.

raised slightly from the surface on which it stands. Several types of feet and foot rings are shown in this book, but the simplest way of raising your slab-made cylinder can be seen in the drawing above. The circlet of clay should be attached to the base by scoring and adding slip in the usual way when the base has hardened a little, and the pot should be left to dry upside down so that the foot ring carries no weight until it is strong enough to do so.

Many beginners want to make pots with lids, and soon confront the difficulty of getting an accurate fit. If a slab cylinder made round a former is sealed off with a top as well as a base, the top and part of the wall can be cut off when the pot has hardened a little. The diagram shows how, by notching the cut and holding the knife pointing downwards, the lid which results will fit well and stay on.

a

The square box

In order to make a square-plan box you will need four sides and a base. Use a set square or a right-angled guide such as an old book to cut the slabs. Having cut one side you can place it upon the rest of the rolled out clay and use it as a template for its twin. The plans **a** and **b** show you the consequences of different arrangements of slabs. If you want to make a pot of square plan by method **b**, two of the sides must be short and two long to compensate for the

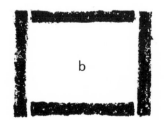

b

Assembling the walls of a slab box around the base.

thickness of the walls. If the slabs are assembled *around* the base as shown in the diagram, this will help to give the pot strength, but the base can be added later, as with the cylinder described above. The pot can be raised by adding a low wall to the base, slightly recessed from the sides, as shown below, or by adding balls of clay to give cushion feet and to raise the pot clear of the table. It is important to attach these cushions adequately by scoring the surface and adding slip, or they will fall off.

A foot which alters the whole concept of the pot is shown left. Bars of clay set across the pot and raising it quite high off the ground are oriental in inspiration, and any museum with a good collection of oriental pottery and porcelain will show the potter how closely the foot of the pot has been studied in the East to reconcile stability with lightness and grace. The cube-like completed slab pot below has been decorated by adding to one of the walls a square of clay into which a seal has been pressed. It is important to note that if you intend to impress a design on the wall itself, this should be done before the slabs are cut out and assembled, as any later pressure will distort the shape of the slab or the pot itself.

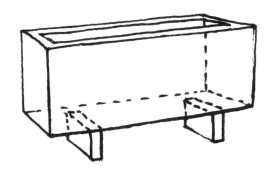

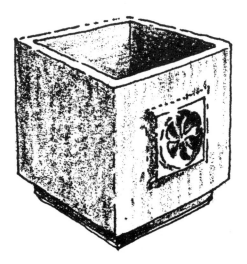

b

a

Lamp base

If the sides of a slab pot taper slightly towards the top, an elegant tower can be made which is a stable form and well suited for use as a lamp base. Study the picture alongside carefully – note how the sides have been chamfered back near the foot, at **a**, and how by positioning the 'collar' of clay strips carefully towards the top of the tower the starkness of the sides has been modified without disturbing the symmetry of the pot. By adding a thin coil or 'worm' of clay around the underside of the collar at **b**, the projecting ledge can be given a graceful concave curve on its lower side. If the pot is to be used for a lamp, then a top must be added with a hole cut into it large enough to accommodate the tapered cork of a lamp adaptor. Cut a square of clay for the top and find the centre by scoring lines from corner to corner, and make the hole at the intersection. You can cut round a coin for this, or use an apple-corer or a metal canister with sharp edges such as is used for packaging colour films or aspirins. A smaller hole can be made in the side near the base with the point of a pencil, for the electric flex to pass through.

A pot like this can be glazed all over (see Chapter 10) or left with a porous rough surface, for it does not need to hold water, but remember that the base of the pot will scratch furniture, and lamp bases are best with pieces of felt glued to their bottoms.

Finish

If the slabs are left as flat, plane surfaces, try to preserve the sharp edges of the form. The sandpaper which is so useful in smoothing and improving casts from moulds has a disastrous blurring effect on slab pots if used mindlessly to round off corners or to 'smooth' irregularities. Its rounding effect on forms is directly contradictory to the rectilinear quality of slabs. If you seek a very regular smooth surface for a slab pot it would be better to use a burnishing tool made of wood or metal when the clay has dried to the leather-hard stage.

It is tempting, as soon as one has started to use slabs, to think in terms of many-sided pots – odd polygonal shapes or regular figures. Sides can slope inwards or outwards, or both, and the planning of the shape of the sides becomes infinitely complex. Irregular figures are rarely successful. The potter, unless he has a very good sculptural sense, cannot be expected to keep control of the form of a flat-sided pot with many facets, and the angle of the joins when it is no longer a right angle sometimes causes difficulties. The angles of a pentagonal plan, for example, will be difficult to achieve and the result will not be worth the effort. The use of curved surfaces, however, is much more rewarding and they are very much in the nature of clay. The illustration shows one simple form, made of two slabs with a base, bulging out in the centre so that the plan of the pot is like an eye. A slab pot of this kind makes a very attractive flower holder. The next illustration shows a more complicated form which happily solves the problem of stability in a narrow shape. Its curving plan makes it difficult to upset. Extra care must be taken to keep the edges crisp and those edges which abut and join have to be cut to the correct angle before any construction begins. The best way to obtain this angle is to draw up a plan of the base.

It is not always necessary for slabs to join at their ends. The star-shaped form illustrated at the bottom of the page is made by

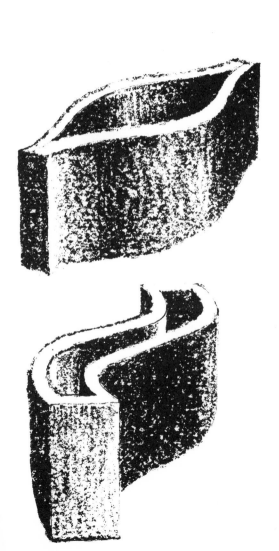

41

scoring and sticking together the curved surfaces of the pot where they touch. If such a vessel is to be used to hold water, a very good join is needed and the base, too, must be carefully made to fit.

When you have had a little practice in the use of slabs it is worthwhile to try a symmetrical curved shape without the use of a former. The pot shown in the drawing was made from slabs cut out according to the plans alongside. The slab has a textured pattern made by a comb or knife before it was curved around, and the edges are scored and joined not by abutting but by overlapping. No attempt is made to hide the overlap, only to ensure that it is firm and continuous. The base is slightly 'dished' so that the pot is not too squat, and the foot ring is sure to be an appropriate size as it relates exactly to the size of the top. This little pot, if well finished and appropriately glazed, can be a delight. It should not be handled more than necessary in the making process or it will look 'fingered' and will lose its clean distinctive lines.

Slab potting is one of the techniques the beginner in pottery can carry out most successfully, but I hope it will already be clear that there is tremendous scope for invention, and it is not surprising that many leading potters use this method and no other for their work.

Slabs of clay lend themselves to sculptural work, as shown **right**.

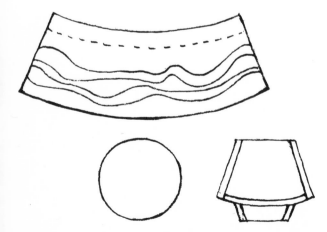

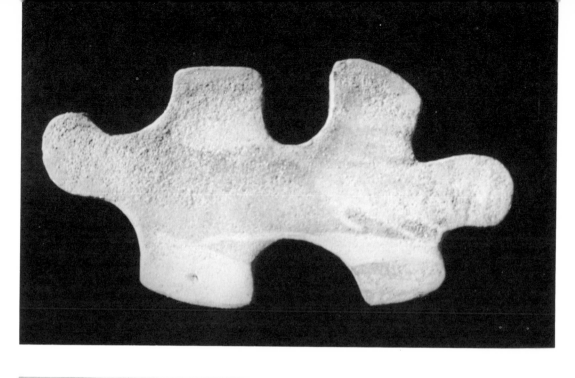

7 Coil Pots

Some people are natural 'coilers' and some of the best coil pots are made by those to whom it is the normal way to make pottery – notably potters from West Africa and the Pueblo Indians of North America. Like slab building, coiling is a simple technique, yet I have seen many beginners struggling unhappily with a sagging mis-shapen vase surrounded by wet worms of clay. They are not enjoying themselves in the least, and they are probably not sure why they are making a pot in this apparently absurd fashion. This is a pity, for the technique allows fine robust work to be made on a scale quite beyond the beginner on the wheel.

Instead of making a pot by erecting sides as in slab pottery, or using a form as in moulds, or a centrifuge as with a wheel, the walls of a coil pot are developed much as a hollow shape is made by coiling down a rope on the deck of a ship, where each loop of rope lies directly above the last. The sides rise and the shape of the sides depends on how each coil lies above its neighbour. The potter can control this precisely and make a large pot of almost any shape. He will use short lengths of clay, rather than a continuous rope, and will probably make a better pot if he lays the coils as rings, one above the other, rather than as a continuous upward spiral. There is nothing sacred or magical about the sausage-like coil shape – the rings themselves often disappear in the texturing of the surface of the pot, and the pot is often stronger if the coil joins do not show. It is not a swift method of

Coiling is an ancient technique. This vessel with ribbed finger decoration and lugs was made in England nearly 3000 years ago.

45

making pottery, but it offers great freedom of design and a size which is limited only by the size of the kiln in which the pot will be fired.

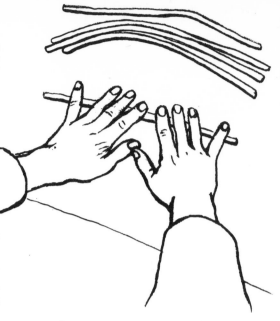

Technique

Prepare clay by wedging in the normal way, and cover the lump with polythene to avoid its drying out. Take off a small piece and roll this out with a rolling pin to the thickness of about one centimetre. Cut this to the shape of the base of the pot – preferably circular – by cutting with a knife round an object of convenient size, such as a small saucer or a beer mat. It is important that the base should not stick to the working surface, so place it on a cloth, a piece of thick paper, or a layer of sand. It helps if the pot can be turned around while working, otherwise the potter has to work round the pot, which takes a lot of space. A revolving metal disk called a bench whirler or banding wheel in ceramic catalogues is ideal and is shown in the drawings, though an improvised working surface that can be turned, such as an inverted plastic bucket will suffice.

When making the coils, aim your hands slightly towards each other. By doing this the coil you make will have a round cross-section, not an oval one.

Having made the base, take more clay from the prepared lump and roll it under the hands as shown above, to produce a sausage about one centimetre in diameter. Try to roll an even 'coil' and do not attempt to make each one longer than you can span with your two hands. As the sausage gets thinner it gets longer, and you should break off whatever runs out beyond the span of your hands. This is not wasted: it can all be used to make coils and short ones are often very useful. When you have made about a dozen coils you can start work. It is pointless to make more, as they dry very quickly when on the work bench and they must be used while they are still entirely flexible – you can make more when

Placing the first coil.

The texture on the surface of the pot will depend on the tool that you use.

you have used up the first batch. Score the edge of the base with a sharp tool and squeeze a little water or slip into the score marks, then press down the first ring of clay on to this roughened edge. Add more rings without any scoring or wetting between surfaces, as the pressure of the fingers on the top of each coil (which will become oval in cross-section) should hold the coils together. When you have added four or five rings the wall of the pot will be beginning to appear and you can strengthen the contact between coils, at the same time as you are improving and smoothing the surface, by using a modelling tool, or your finger, or a cardboard comb which will drag clay from one coil to another and create a surface which is as rough or as smooth as you like. It is as well to do this on both the inside and the outside of the pot, as the diagram shows. Now add another four or five rings and repeat the linking process.

Shapes and sizes

The thickness of the wall is governed by the thickness of the coil; large pots need thick walls, and conversely small pots need thin ones, but I do not advise you to make a small coil pot. It is a waste of time: it takes just as long to make a small one as a large one, because thin walls made with miserable little coils gain height very slowly. I suggest coils one centimetre in diameter (or about the thickness of your little finger): this size creates a wall half as thick again when the coils are pressed down and will ensure that you make something fairly substantial in size. Other methods already described – slab building and pinching – are more suited to small shapes, and moulding is more sensible for flat or shallow shapes.

Think in terms of tall or 'full' shapes when using coils and try to avoid the temptation to coil a pot with an oval, triangular or irregular plan. You cannot coil a circular-sectioned pot with perfect symmetry like a pot made on a wheel or a lathe, and it is a mistake slavishly to attempt to do so, but coils are more at home going round, and a pot which looks like a tomato or turnip can be a fine handsome shape. It is less likely to look well if it has ins and

outs like a potato. The photograph on page 50 shows how well a bulging shape can look, even on the top of a cylindrical form, provided it is kept generous and full. Building was most difficult where this pot bellies out above the shoulder. A coil pot is made to swell if the superimposed rings of clay are made progressively larger, but the downward pressure of unsupported clay is great and beginners may find that swelling shapes collapse before their eyes. It is best to begin by constructing a vertical, gently tapering shape as shown in the drawing alongside. If changes of profile are kept to a minimum, the emphasis will be on the surface and on the termination of the shape. Sometimes beginners who cope well with the construction have difficulty in finishing the pot and go on and on upwards like a knitter unable to turn the heel of a sock. Sometimes, too, beginners will feel after an hour or so of work that their pot looks pointless and undistinguished. Imagine just the bottom half of the pot on page 50 – it would look dull and incomplete. The important thing is to keep the finished form in mind at all stages and also to remember the maximum height of the kiln. It is very, very annoying to make a pot which pleases you only to find that it will not fit into the kiln.

A marked change of direction will help to give the pot the emphasis it needs for its top and it is easier to make this if it turns inwards, as in the photograph opposite, for the clay will hold itself up like the dome of a building. If you want the shape to turn outwards, the problems of bellying and collapse already mentioned will crop up, and a simple answer is to use scaffolding. Strips of clay slightly harder than those used for making the pot will prop up the vulnerable parts, and can be removed as your pot hardens and dries. The clay will dry as you work, over a period of two hours, and the bottom part of your pot, luckily, will become hard enough for you to handle it without squashing the pot as a whole if it needs to be moved out of the way for finishing another

Right: *the better the junction between the coils, the stronger the pot. Blend coils together on the inside of the pot as well as the outside whenever you can.*

time. An incomplete coil pot can be covered with an airtight polythene bag one week for finishing the next.

Like pots made by other methods, coil pots will be judged by their rims, so the final coils are very important. A degree of unevenness in the level of the wall is bound to develop as the sides rise and this can be corrected at the rim so that the top is level, or at least decisive. A short length of coil tapering to a point at both ends added to only part of a circuit will fill up any 'lows', and if there is a 'high' it can simply be cut away with a knife. Sometimes an extra thick coil on the top helps to give the rim emphasis. The diagrams on page 53 show how very slight variations in the treatment of the rim can change the character of the whole.

If the top is important to the character of the coil pot, so is the base. The tapering form illustrated on page 48 has a simple plain base like a milk bottle. A bulging form may look dumpy, however, if its bottom is very wide and a swelling shape which will not collapse can be made by coiling the lower part of the pot inside some kind of mould – the inside of a kitchen mixing bowl is a good one. The diagram shows how this is done. The mould first should be dusted with chalk or greased to prevent sticking. A single round coil, added when the complete pot is taken out of the mould, will make a stable foot ring.

Below: *using a bowl to support a coil pot.* **Right**: *temporary scaffolding made of hard clay to prevent an open shape from collapsing.*

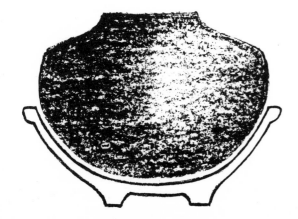

Surface and decoration

The surface of a coil pot is absolutely vital to its success. Try to match a texture to the form of the pot. Finger and modelling-tool marks make a rough texture, and are not easy on the hands when the pot is fired, but attractive when thickly glazed. The same marks gently patted down with a flat piece of wooden battening give a very different texture. A coarse tooth comb made of cardboard or a fine-toothed pocket comb will score the surface. A hacksaw blade will leave fine scratches and has the added advantage, being bendy, of curving easily around the body of the pot. Sandpaper used on the pot when dry will smooth it like a pebble, and a wooden burnisher rubbed over a pot when nearly dry will create a shiny waxy surface which often remains after the pot is fired. There is also the opportunity for cutting or decorating the surface, as described in the chapter on slab pottery. Stamps and seals have to be pressed in with caution as the walls lose their appeal if they are pushed in even slightly, and a hand must be placed on the inside to support the wall when pressing on the outside. Raised decoration can be successful if it does not disrupt the form, and handles, ears, lugs and knobs can be added easily, as the drawing shows.

Handles and lugs added to coil pots can serve a decorative as well as a practical purpose.

Golden rules

1. Coil pots are made from plastic clay wedged as described in Chapter 2. Do not use water, or anything wet when placing one coil on another. Avoid stickiness in the working area and keep your hands and fingers dry.

2. Make sure that the rings of clay are properly bonded together with pressure from the fingers or tools on both sides of the wall. Inadequately bonded pots or those made from different kinds of clay may well fall apart when they are dry or leak after they are fired and glazed. If you are pleased with a robust coil pot, you will probably want it to be watertight, for coil pots often look very handsome when filled with flowers.

Coiling gives the potter the freedom of the sculptor which is why coil pottery – though using a simple technique – is the most difficult kind of pottery to do really well. The further one strays from the simple shape the greater the problems.

Just where you place the final coil, and how you treat it, makes a great difference to the finished result. The variations **right** *show some suggested profiles.*

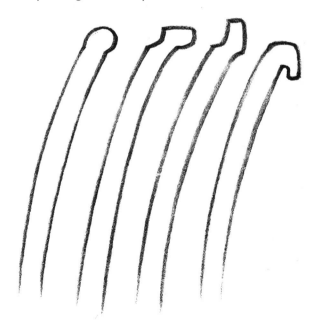

8 Shapes on the Wheel

Opinions vary among teachers about the stage at which the beginner should start work on the wheel, but most would-be potters want to try the wheel as soon as they possibly can. It is the key instrument which allows symmetrical bowls and cylinders to be made quickly, as if by magic, and it is my view that the wheel gives students an understanding of the capacity and limits of clay quicker than any other form of pottery making.

The principles of working on the wheel can be expressed simply and briefly, but the full technique is a complex one and beyond the scope of an outline guide to pottery. For this reason this chapter concentrates on all you need to know to make simple shapes. When you want to go further you must consult an experienced teacher or a more detailed book.

Craftsmen often make identical pots by drawing up a ring of clay from the centre of a large revolving lump on the wheel. The lump gets smaller as the pots so made are cut off the top and eventually it is replaced with another one. A more normal beginning for pottery students is to centre a small lump of clay on the wheel and to use it all to make one pot. How large a lump should you start with? I suggest that it should be the size of one of your fists when clenched – such a piece of clay will weigh about 500 grams. Shape the clay into a ball and press it down on to a stationary wheel head, making sure that both your hands and the wheel are dry. You will either be using an electrically or pedal powered wheel, and you want to get up a good head of speed to help you to centre the clay. The absolute necessity for this piece of clay to be running true will become apparent as soon as you begin. If the clay wobbles, the pot will wobble out of control. Wet your hands from a bowl of water within reach, spill some water over the clay to act as a lubricant and, using both hands, press hard down on the clay. Concentrate on holding your hands still while the clay and the wheel revolve. There is no set position for the hands – lock them together and in a comfortable position and try to keep your elbows on the rim which surrounds the wheel framework. If the clay refuses to spin truly under your hands then try using a softer piece. The long battle that some beginners have with the centering process can be shortened if they start with clay that is very soft indeed. This will be too soft for successful pot-making, but it can easily be centred. When you have done this, try again with a harder piece, and practise until you can cope with a lump of clay hard enough for throwing. If you can hold your hands steadily on the clay, and take them away gently, the revolving mound is ready to be made hollow.

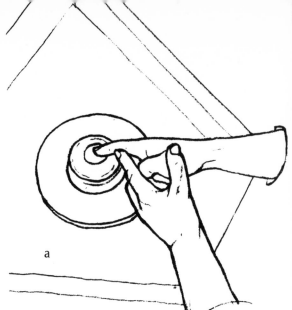

a

*Make a hollow in the middle of the centred ball of clay (**a**) and enlarge the hollow with the thumbs (**b**).*

Ashtray

For many years I have tried to prevent students from making ashtrays. This was nothing to do with smoking, but was because the decision to make an ashtray so often came towards the end of making an unsuccessful vase, when all that was left revolving on the wheel was the base and a ragged low wall. A successful ashtray made on the wheel will be plain, heavy in the base and short in the wall. It is much more likely that a beginner will be able to achieve this than a graceful tall vase. If the ashtray is the basic intention, then I would encourage you to make one as follows.

Approach your perfectly centred piece of clay with the right index finger and, with the wheel revolving quite fast, find the very centre in order to make a hollow, as shown in the diagram (**a**). Put both thumbs into the hollow and press downwards to widen and deepen this navel in the clay until it is the size of a tennis ball (**b**).

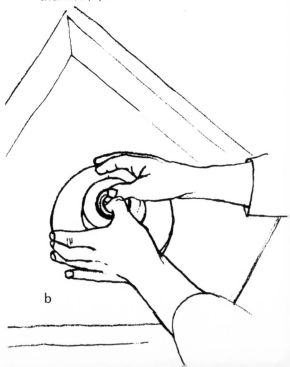

b

Then remove the thumbs carefully and slowly. The rim around this hollowed out cup will probably be rough and uneven. Use the index finger of your right hand as a scraper by pressing it down firmly on the rim, angled slightly downwards (**c**). It should

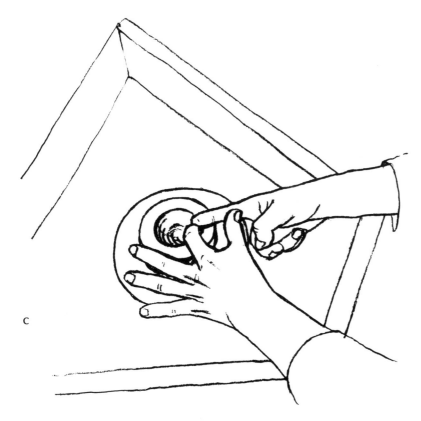

c

*Hold the index finger of your right hand firmly and press it on to the top of the hollow bowl (**c**). It will flatten and widen the rim.*

level out the top, though it may push some unwanted clay back into the hollow cup. With the wheel revolving, use a sponge to clean up the inside and the top and take a look at the side of your pot. It will probably have a profile not unlike the shaded edge to the cross-section right. This can be cut back to the black outline in the diagram by holding a metal straight-edge against the clay as shown in **d**. The heavier the metal the better. It does not need to

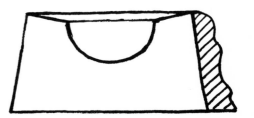

have a sharp edge, but any snags on its edge will make horizontal marks around your pot. With the wheel still revolving, clean the pot over with a damp sponge, removing any sticky clay which may lie alongside the pot on top of the wheel head. The ashtray is now ready to be cut off the wheel, and this should be done by pulling a nylon or metal cord carefully under the pot as shown in the drawing **e**. The pot may move slightly away from the centre of the wheel when this cut is made, or it may stay firmly in place. If the latter, then sprinkle some water on the wheel head and draw the cord through again, pulling some of the water with it. This will almost certainly loosen the pot and you will be able to slide it with two fingers of one hand, held near to its base, on to a smooth wet surface alongside. The best material on to which to slide your pot is a glazed tile. These are very easy to come by and work well provided the surface is absolutely smooth. Having safely delivered the ashtray on its tile to a shelf for drying, you should run the nylon cord under the pot again so that it does not stick firmly to the tile as it dries.

This simple pot has tremendous advantages. It is an appropriate weight (heavy) for its function, and it can be made to a high degree of precision by someone with very little experience in pottery and without hours of practice on the wheel.

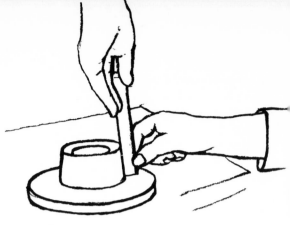

d

*Use a ruler or turning tool with a straight edge to make the profile of the ashtray (**d**). Cut the ashtray free with the nylon cord (**e**) and push it off the wheel head by using only the fingertips, to avoid marking the pot.*

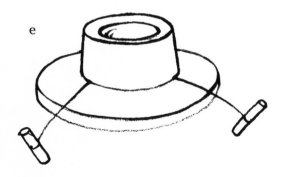

e

A bowl

'A set of soup bowls.' Nearly every beginner, it seems, wants to make bowls by the dozen, or at least the half-dozen. Abandon the project. It is not difficult to make a bowl, but for a beginner to attempt to make several identical units on the wheel is an absurd waste of time. Moulds give you the opportunity of repeating shapes exactly. If you want soup bowls in sets, refer to Chapter 5. The basic bowl shape, however, is not a bad one for a beginner to learn, provided that he does not try to make one that is too large.

The diagrams **a**, **b** and **c** show what happens to the clay in cross-section. As for the ashtray, with the wheel rotating near its maximum speed, make a depression in the centred clay with one or two thumbs, and press down until your fingers and your eyes tell you that you are near enough to the base. A thickness of one centimetre is a good one, but you can only check this after you have made the pot.

Without withdrawing the thumbs from the hole in the clay, push *away* and upwards in a steady curve. This should produce a cross-section as shown in **b.** Now is the time to use the two hands separately, and to reduce the speed of the wheel by about a half. The fingers of the left hand are used inside the pot, with the fingertips near the curve of the bowl and the hand leaning towards the right. The right hand will support the outside of the bowl and the two hands drawn up steadily together will both raise and widen the shape as shown in **c.**

One of the most difficult positions for the beginner to learn is the angle of the outside, right, hand. It is 'knuckled over' so that only the left-hand side of the index finger is in contact with the pot, as the photograph on page 61 shows. Try to adopt this position without contortions. It is a sensitive position but remember that it is better to hold your hands in a relaxed way than to follow a rule which may, for you, be uncomfortable and may inhibit you from shaping the pot.

An expert thrower will draw the bowl out to its final shape by repeating this action two or three times. A beginner may well

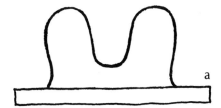

a

b

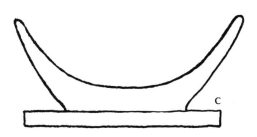

c

59

want to do it again and again, and the pot will probably collapse as the clay becomes fatigued. It is better for the beginner to settle for the shape shown in diagram **c** and to concentrate on the evenness of the rim and the smoothness of the inside. If the original hollow in your pot was not quite central the pot will have wobbled, perhaps to its ruin. It is better to begin again than to try to redeem an off-centre pot. You may find that although the pot appears to be running true there is a tendency for one side to rise higher than the other. The unevenness will get worse unless you cut the top level. This is done, quite easily, with the wheel revolving at the same steady speed as for making the pot. You press a pin, attached for convenience to a cork, through the wall of the clay from the outside about one centimetre below the top. You *hold the pin steady with its tip projecting through the inside wall until it has completed at least one revolution*, then you gently raise the pin, and lift the uneven ring of clay with it. The diagram shows this action in progress. It is as well to practise. When you have learnt it, it is useful and quite enjoyable. Many beginners mistrust the pin and stab at the clay, buckling the pot. They may be uneasy about cutting tops level and be tempted to leave a pot with an uneven rim.

The rim is the most important part of a small bowl, and it should be smoothed with a fingertip, a sponge or a strip of chamois leather. The inside of the bowl, too, must be mopped up with a sponge to dry the pool of water which has accumulated there in the making. Use the sponge firmly and you may flatten out some of the ridges and furrows in the clay. Remember to do all these things with the wheel revolving steadily. Do not stop the wheel until the bowl is quite complete.

Before cutting the bowl free with the wire, as for the ashtray, use your right index finger against the outside of the bowl, pointing downwards towards the centre of the wheel, to trim away some of the unwanted clay which clutters up the base. Sponge or scrape the outer part of the wheel head free of clay and slip and you will be able the more easily to guide your pot on to a waiting wet tile when it is loosened by the wire.

Right: the positions of the hands when making a bowl.

Cutting off an uneven rim with a pin attached to a cork.

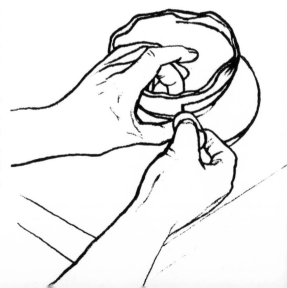

Take a good look at your bowl from above and from the side. If it is uneven or unpleasing at this time, then you are never going to like it very much. Why not cut it vertically through the centre with a wire? This will destroy it, but it will give you the chance to look at the cross-section of the wall. If you are not happy with the pot this is probably because the walls are uneven and your next effort must be to apply a very even pressure in drawing out this shape. The more graceful the curve of the bowl, the more you will like it. Try to aim at a single curve, not a complex one.

When the pot is leather hard after a day or so of drying in normal temperatures, you can handle it without damaging it. Take it off its tile and turn it upside down. The bottom can be trimmed by placing the bowl on centre, upside down on the wheel head, to cut off the surplus clay. It is an attractive but fairly complex technique called turning, and a bowl being turned is shown in the photograph opposite.

It is important to fix your bowl firmly to the wheel head by its rim without damaging it, and most metal wheel heads have concentric circles cut into their surface which helps you to position the bowl correctly. It should be held in position by knobs of clay pressed against both rim and wheel head, and these pieces of clay must be neither so soft that they stick to the pot nor so hard that they damage it by distorting the shape of the rim. A complete even ring of clay pressed on to the wheel head makes a good 'bed' for the bowl to rest on, and by cutting a groove in this ring of clay with the point of a turning tool as the wheel revolves you can easily provide yourself with a guide line for centering the pot.

Turning is a process that frequently seems to take up a disproportionate amount of beginners' time in the workshop or class. In some factories the 'turners' are responsible for the most creative part of pot production, for they make the shape of the pot on a lathe, but beginners should regard it as a matter of tidying up and keep it to a minimum. The bowl on page 64, if it is to function well and not feel too heavy in the hand, should have its profile **a** changed to the profile shown in **b**, and this can only be done with the bowl upside down, by turning.

A bowl being turned on the wheel. In this instance the bowl is wider than the wheel head, and the plugs of clay which hold it on cannot be seen as they are beneath the rim. The turning tool must be held steadily when it is used to remove clay from the foot of a pot. Notice how the left hand steadies the tool near its cutting tip.

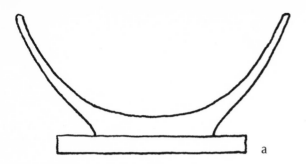

a

b

Having fixed the bowl in the centre of the wheel head, check it for being correctly placed by incising a ring near to the edge of the base of the pot with the wheel revolving. If this circle corresponds neatly with the edge of the pot and does not swerve towards or away from it, you can start work. If your incised circle is eccentric to the pot then you must correct it. Loosen the clay supports, and move the bowl in the direction shown in the diagram. This will bring the incised ring and the rim of the bowl into a better relationship. Replace the wedges and try the pot again for centre by incising another ring. Like centering the clay before throwing a pot on the wheel, this positioning process is absolutely essential. Persevere until you get it right.

With the heavy metal turning tool illustrated on page 15, you will remove clay from the centre of the base and from the outside of the base, leaving a small foot ring on which the pot stands. Mark the position of the foot ring as the wheel revolves with two more incised circles made with the point of the tool, and then, using the sharp blade of the tool, cut away the leather-hard clay on both sides of the foot ring, starting with the outside. The photograph on page 63 shows how the tool is held, the left hand supporting the head of the tool near the blade, and the angle of the blade being more or less a radius to the pot. It is better to hold the tool at an oblique angle from your sitting position, making a digging action, than an acute angle with a dragging action, as the latter will cause ugly ripple or 'chatter' marks as the tool bounces off the clay. A little practice will familiarize the beginner with both tools and technique.

A pot is not centred if a ring cut in its base as the wheel revolves does not correspond with the edge of the base itself. To put this right, move the pot slightly in the direction of the arrows.

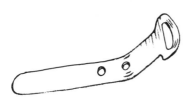

*Curve the 'eye' of a metal cable clip, as used by electricians, and you have a ready-made tool for fluting the outside of a pot, as shown **above**.*

Do not cut too much away. You can all too easily go through the base of your bowl if you cut it too deeply, but try to remember and to copy the shape you have made inside the bowl when you are turning the outside. This will ensure that the walls of the bowl have an even thickness.

Some beginners find turning rather an ordeal. It is nice to do it well, but it is rather like polishing the soles of your shoes – if the uppers are nothing to write home about, then no one is going to take the trouble to examine them, and if they *do* look underneath, your diligence will only draw attention to the shabby top. It is a good general rule that no bowl is *redeemed* by turning. It may be improved, but it is in the throwing stage that quality is set.

Further cutting can be done to decorate the bowl while the pot is leather hard. Vertical 'flutes' can be made as on the pot shown left, using a wire fluting tool which can be bought, or made from a metal clip. The key factor in the tidying and decorating processes is the state of the clay. The clay of a leather-hard pot will, of course, not stick to the hands. Neither will it give to gentle pressure, but it will tear easily, like a processed cheese, and not flakily like, say, a chocolate bar. If a pot has dried to beyond the leather-hard stage or begun to lighten in colour with drying, there is not much point in trying to turn it, although sandpaper is quite useful to tidy it up when it is bone dry.

A great number of beginners break their pots when they are at the leather-hard stage or drier. The clay has no strength until it has been fired and so-called 'green' pots must be handled with the greatest care, and *never* picked up by their rims.

Cylinders and upright shapes

'Throw cylinders' is a piece of advice to the potter not unlike 'practise' to a budding pianist or an ice skater. It means slog away and you will improve. Unfortunately for the ambitious beginner, who may find cylinders boring, it is good advice. A cylinder is a harmonious shape, but its value in throwing is not as an end in itself but because it provides the basic shape from which more complex curved pots are made.

Unlike all the other techniques and objects described up to this point in the book, the cylinder is not an easy project for the beginner, and failure to begin with is more likely than success. Provide yourself with several small balls of clay of similar size, for you will need them all.

Centre the clay as for the ashtray, and press the thumbs into a hollow in the middle of the hump as before. This time, however, you should press the thumbs away from the body so that an open flat floor is made inside the cavern in the clay. Keeping the thumbs inside the clay, and with the wheel revolving quite fast, use the fingers, which are all on the outside of the shape, to grasp the form from the outside. The clay which lies between the fingers and thumbs will rise up to form the wall of your cylinder. Taking away the hands from the clay carefully and slowly, you should now reduce the speed of the wheel and put one hand inside and one hand outside the clay. Your hand may seem rather large to fit inside the pot and you may do better to insert only as many fingers as you can without distorting the shape, drawing up the wall is illustrated alongside. The tendency is for the clay to throw itself into a wider and wider shape, which is why the small bowl already described is easier to make than the cylinder, as it is a natural shape for the clay. You may find that your cylinder wants to look like a plant pot – wider at the top than the bottom. This tendency can be controlled by compressing the clay from the outside. It should be done with both hands, as if throttling the clay, and it is important that the hands should be wet with water for this operation, as for all actions in throwing on the wheel. Too harsh a compression will make the rim ripple and frill, the walls spiral and twist, and the cylinder collapse. Too little force and nothing at all will be achieved. You have to experiment until you find how much pressure the clay can take from outside. The photograph on page 76 shows batches of cylinders in the making.

If you apply pressure to the walls evenly, if you draw your hands up the clay at a steady speed and keep the wheel revolving slowly,

Drawing up the wall of a cylinder.

you should be able to control the clay. When your hands reach the top of the wall remove them very gently from the clay, as a rapid jerky action may throw the pot off centre.

By applying more pressure on the inside wall the clay will respond by bellying outwards. Closing it again by collaring or throttling as already described is harder work, but it is by this balance of forces that a cylindrical shape is changed into a round shape, such as the pot illustrated on page 67.

If you want to see results from your first efforts on the wheel, then do not attempt to use too much clay, or make too large a pot. The technique of throwing complex shapes contains so many nuances that the beginner can easily become confused or overawed. Observe the following rules and you should enjoy the experience.

1. Keep hands wet.

2. Keep movements smooth and slow.

3. Slow the speed of the wheel as your pot progresses.

4. Discard any pot which wobbles out of centre, and start again.

5. Do not try to make the walls too thin, especially near the bottom of the pot.

A neat and trim cylinder or upright shape will not need turning when it is leather hard, as was necessary with the bowl, but you can remove the rough edge from the base by chamfering it with the fingernail or a knife before the clay has become too dry.

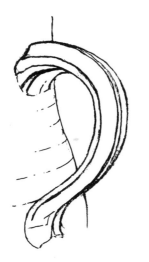

Handles

Handles are loops of clay through which fingers can be hooked to pick up a pot. Many simple pots need handles. Museums showing medieval and even prehistoric pottery will show more eloquently than many modern manufacturers of pottery that a pulled handle – a plug of clay drawn out by pulling with a moist hand into a carrot shape which is then bent over and attached to the pot by both its head and foot – makes a natural arch which often complements the pot. Pulling handles in this way takes practice, and it is a pity to spoil a well-made hollow form by adding a graceless lumpy handle. Two simple but often less aesthetically pleasing methods of making handles are slicing a thrown cylinder into rings and pressing one ring against the side of the pot, or taking a wire shaped as the diagram below shows and pulling it through a prepared block of clay, so that an even-diameter bar of clay is cut free which can then be bent and attached to the pot by its two ends.

Above: *a pulled handle and,* **below**, *alternative methods of handle-making.*

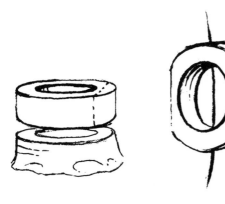

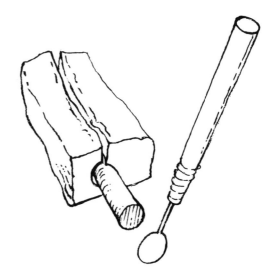

9 Decoration

Some people have a flair for decorating pots, for transforming the bland but complicated three-dimensional shape of a thrown or coiled pot into an object which crackles with excitement, often borne of strong contrasts of pattern and tone.

The desire to decorate the surface of a pot goes back a long way – the pot shown opposite was made by a Keresan Indian in New Mexico, and illustrates the marriage of design and form, of utility and beauty. Decoration can be complex and representational, as on many of the pots of Classical Greece or Renaissance Italy, or simple and abstract as on many oriental pots. It certainly is not only associated with painting – many of the techniques already described for incising, impressing and applying clay are decorative techniques, and of course some features of a pot, such as handles, are both functional and decorative.

Beginners often seek rules for decorating pots, and a problem for a teacher is that the formulation and observance of rules often removes the vitality that a beginner with a bold idea can bring to a pot. Thus the only rule that I intend to give in this book is: be bold. More pots are spoiled by tentative design than are damaged by abrupt and firm patterns. It helps if you can think of the decoration of your pot whilst you are making its fabric. Patterns which are applied as an afterthought are often better not applied at all. The decoration combed or incised into the sides of a coil pot during its making usually combines happily with the form.

Pueblo Indian pot, finely coiled and boldly decorated with slip.

71

Vignettes applied with a paintbrush after firing are less often successful. Beginners who want to paint a primrose, or a horse jumping a gate, on to the curving shoulder of a vase are really asking for trouble, although it *can* be successful. Satyrs and nymphs dance around Greek kylixs on floors that are, if anything, spherical, and painted octopuses, stylized or realistic, cling to the surface of many pots made in the Mediterranean region. The secret is in a harmony between pattern and shape, and this is too nebulous a description, I am afraid, to be much help to the beginner. I hope that the pot illustrated opposite, which was made some 4000 years ago in Greece, will illustrate what I mean. The zig-zag pattern painted on in black and the small vessels which cluster around the sides – probably receptacles for oil, not candles – are both part of the function and of the decoration of this pot.

Decoration using coloured slip

Decoration with slip is recommended for beginners. It depends basically upon a contrast of colour between the body clay of the pot and the slip which is added to it. Sometimes more than one slip will be used and the colour and tonal range further increased. Slip for decoration is the same material as for casting or for cementing joints, as described on page 27. It is clay and water mixed to a consistency of thin cream and darkened in colour by the addition of powdered metal oxides. Slip is applied to a raw unfired pot and both body clay and slip clay, therefore, have to go into the kiln together. It is important that they expand and contract at the same rate in response to heat so that the slip does not crack off. The simplest way of ensuring this is to use the body clay itself with an addition of water to make a slip. A red body clay can be turned into a black slip by adding cobalt oxide in the proportion of 5 per cent to the dry weight of the clay, while a total of 5 per cent of cobalt and copper in equal parts added to a white clay will make a blue-green slip. Iron oxide alone makes brown, and 10 per cent of iron oxide added to the blue-green slip will

Opposite: *ceremonial vessel made in Greece about 2000* BC. *Light coloured clay, painted with black slip.*

72

make a black slip that can be used on white bodies. If you want to use a white slip on top of coloured clay, or on top of a coloured slip, then you should mix powdered ball clay with 20 per cent china clay (for whiteness), adding a little feldspar if tests show that the white slip does not adhere to the basic clay. All these materials are readily available from ceramic suppliers, and with the exception of cobalt oxide are cheap to buy. They should certainly all be available in an evening institute pottery workshop.

Coloured slip can be painted directly on to an unfired pot with a paintbrush, and it is important to do this when the body clay of the pot is hard, but not completely dry. The surface of the clay will absorb water very quickly and a large floppy-headed brush is necessary. The bristles must be soft, as stiff ones leave ugly scratch marks on the pot. Indeed the choice or availability of the right brush is crucial to the success of a painted design. You cannot satisfactorily 'go over' a pattern painted in slip, as the additional brush marks will show when the pot has been fired, and the best results come from making single marks with a brush that is big enough for a bold design. The simple designs shown below, or any other bold patterns, can be made with dark slip on the inside of a shallow bowl using a brush of the correct shape, shown right. They

Right: *feathering is a traditional technique of decoration using contrasting slips. Lines of white slip piped from a slip trailer into a wet ground of coloured slip are drawn into shapes like the patterns on a bird's wing by running a bristle, or any fine point, across the stripes in alternate directions.*

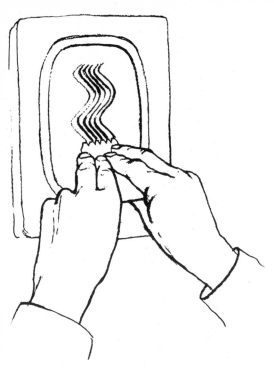

Incising a design with a cardboard comb.

Left: *throwing cylinders on the wheel.*

can also be made into light designs on a darkened ground by flooding the bowl first with dark slip, pouring the surplus out, and then cutting back to the ground below. The best tool for this is a sharp blade set like a traction hoe, at right angles to its handle. The technique of sgraffito involves scratching through a dark slip to the ground beneath with a fine point. The drawing shows how a cardboard comb can be used to incise a bold design through a slipped surface to the clay below.

On flat surfaces – for example, on the lid of the slabbed container drawn on page 38 – the technique can be reversed by using a lino cutting tool to engrave a design – perhaps an initial letter – into the body clay. If the surface is then coated with a stiff mixture of coloured slip, which must completely fill the engraved design, and the surface scraped back when the slip has dried, the design will appear again as a coloured inlay.

A coloured stain such as cobalt oxide can be applied, not with slip but simply mixed with water, to an incised design by sponging it on to the pot when the pot is dry, and then immediately sponging it away again with clean water. The oxide will stay in the cracks of the incised design and show strongly when the pots have been put in the kiln. Avoid using too much water, however, or the outside of the unfired pot will suffer.

Slip trailing

A light design on a dark ground can be made by adding white slip through a 'slip trailer', rather as icing is piped on to a cake. The slip trailer consists of a rubber bulb with a nozzle, as shown in the diagram overleaf and the colour photograph on page 75. A plastic ketchup container or mustard dispenser makes an excellent substitute. The slip used in the trailer should be stiffer than that used for the ground. White slip piped from a trailer into a ground of damp dark slip does not sink completely into the background but stays slightly proud, even when the vessel is tapped to get the design to 'set' into the background. The diagram shows how a slip trailer can be used to make a bold calligraphic abstract design in a press-moulded dish. It can also, of course, be used to make a figurative design, and many historic slip-decorated dishes celebrate events and people with lively realism. Different coloured slips are reluctant to mix naturally into one another, and decorative advantage can be taken of this by 'marbling', spiral and other effects being achieved by holding the mould containing the clay body and wet slip in a vertical position and twisting it vigorously so that gravity pulls the slip into interlocking shapes. The colour photograph on page 75 shows a dish in a press mould being decorated by feathering. A series of parallel lines of white slip are trailed across a coloured slip ground from a slip trailer, and a fine point (in this case a bristle) is then drawn at right angles across the lines so that it drags the slip into bracket-like shapes reminiscent of the patterns on a bird's wing.

Paper patterns

Another method of making contrasting designs using slip is to fix a paper pattern to the surface of the leather-hard pot before the slip is added. A star-shaped piece of thin paper, stuck with a little water to the inside of an unfired bowl, can be pulled away when the slip layer has been applied leaving a bare clay star exposed. The results by this method are often not very precise but slip is a wandering, random medium of decoration anyway and irregularities at the edge of the design are often in keeping with the material. Paper patterns or natural objects such as leaves can be placed above one layer of slip and under a second so that the decorative possibilities of this method are increased.

Another form of negative patterning which is very popular is painting with wax. A mixture of warm candle wax and turpentine, or furniture wax heated so that it flows freely, can be painted on to the clay surface. Slip poured on to this will be repelled by the wax and the painted design will later burn away in the kiln leaving a bare area in the shape of the wax pattern. As this is such a **widespread technique, especially in small potteries producing** large numbers of closely similar pots, it cannot be left out of any

Slip, squeezed through the nozzle of a slip trailer, behaves exactly like icing piped on to a cake. The designs can be intricate, or overlapping. Try to avoid making them spidery.

summary of decoration techniques, but it is not recommended for beginners as warm wax is difficult to cope with when all concentration is needed for the design, and the medium is ruinous to brushes.

Slip decorated pots are fired in the kiln when they are bone dry, and then glazed with a transparent glaze if they are to be watertight. Opaque or coloured glazes will, of course, mask the design you have made.

Painted decoration

Much decoration is done after the biscuit firing, using the materials described in the next chapter. The sgraffito technique used with slip can also be used to scratch through the glaze to the clay body beneath, and this is best done before the glaze itself has dried out on the body of the pot – see Chapter 10. Most decoration at this stage, however, is done with a paintbrush, and again it is important to use the right scale of brush for the design you have in mind. Try your design by painting it on to blotting paper first: the dry, biscuit fired pot will soak up the paint in much the same way, and a pot coated with dry, powdered glaze will be even more absorbent. Single isolated marks repeated around a wheel-thrown shape are often more effective if bounded by horizontal bands, and banded decoration is one of the simplest forms to apply accurately. The illustration left shows how, by touching a revolving pot with a steady brush bearing a colouring stain, a fine and perfect circle will be made around the pot. Use either a portable banding wheel or the head of the wheel used for throwing for this – do not try to make horizontal bands on a pot without the means of spinning the pot, for an uneven or near-horizontal line will have a very disruptive effect on the form. Often the best place for bands, especially on a globular pot, is near its shoulder, and the drawing of the elegant jug on page 83 shows how such bands on the neck and throat are supplemented by strong simple vertical forms, linked with curves which emphasize the swelling shape of the pot.

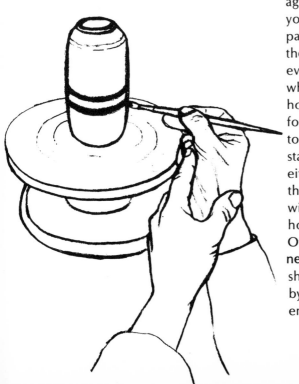

By spinning a pot on the wheel head, perfect horizontal bands can be made by touching the pot with a loaded paintbrush.

*Brush painted design on a vase by Michael Woods and, **right**, painted tile panel by William de Morgan.*

There is no need to copy the decorative styles of the past, but no hand-made pottery made today is decorated with the same vigour and grace as was practised in previous centuries. A visit to a museum with a good ceramic section will help you to decide on the kind of decoration which appeals to you most and lies within your skills.

Left: *simple and effective decoration in brown slip on a pot from Luristan, Persia, 1500* BC. **Right**: *beak-spout jug from Melos, 2000* BC. *Black slip painted on white slip on a brown body.*

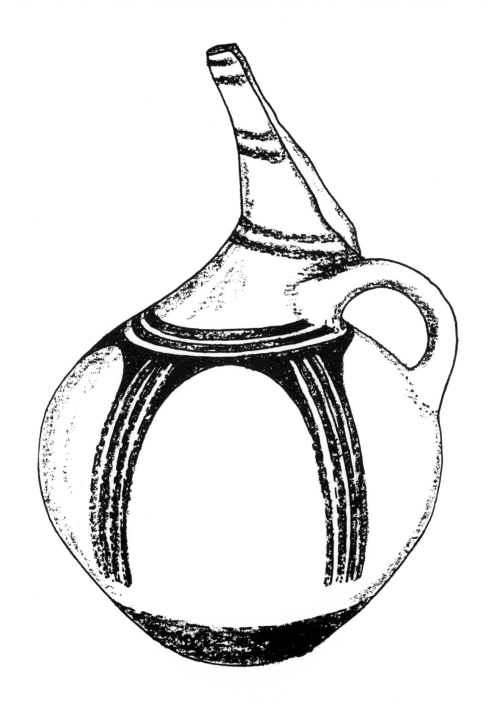

83

10 Glazing

Pots are fired in the kiln when they are bone dry, then covered with glaze and refired to give them a waterproof, coloured and often decorative surface.

It is not easy to get an even coating of powdered glass with no adhesive qualities on to the complicated three-dimensional shape of most pots – even simple cylinders. The normal method is to suspend the powder in water, and in factories this is sprayed on to the pots as a car is sprayed with paint. In a potter's workshop the glaze is kept in a bucket, sieved regularly to make sure that it is well mixed and smooth, and the pots are dipped into it as a piece of fish is dipped in batter. Because it does not stick to the pot like paint, the glaze can easily be rubbed off again with careless handling, and it is not easy to touch up. You cannot apply glaze with a paintbrush as it will not go on evenly, and an even coat is very important.

If you have joined an evening class you will probably find that there are only two glazes available – clear glass and an opaque white. These will be made with silica, with lead or borax as a 'flux' to help melting, and they are non-toxic. If you are potting at home, glaze can be bought quite cheaply as a fine powder in a bag, which should be mixed with water and sieved. Sieving is vital whenever it is to be used as the ingredients are heavy and settle at the bottom very quickly.

Beginners always have difficulty in knowing how thick the

Wheel-made pot by Janet Leach. The arching shapes of light-coloured glaze are made by moving the pot under a thin stream of glaze as it is poured from a jug.

liquid should be, and it is hard to be precise or dogmatic about glaze thickness as glazes vary enormously, and so does the absorbency of the pots to be glazed. The more absorbent the pot the more liquid will soak into its surface when dipped in the glaze, and the thicker the layer of glaze particles left on the surface when the water has soaked into the pot. Although there are practical dangers in glazing too thickly – principally that the glaze will become too mobile when it has melted and will pool inside the pot and run down the outside, sticking the pot permanently to the shelf – it is aesthetically more satisfying if the glaze is thick rather than thin. A thin coat of glaze will look like a mean varnish on the pot when it is fired, and this is what you will get if the glaze in the bucket is watery. If as thick as double cream it is too thick for safety. A teacher will be able to dip his hand into the glaze and say from experience if it is right, but if you do not have his experience to lean on, then try to mix up your glaze like thin cream. Dip a piece of fired clay into it and when it has dried (this will only take half a minute) test the thickness of the powder with your fingernail. If it flakes away very easily and has a thickness of about one millimetre it is probably right. If it does not flake it is too thin, and if your fingernail makes a deep furrow in it, it is too thick.

All glazes are white or pale-coloured, and are opaque on application. Their colours and surfaces develop when they melt. If they are cooled too quickly in the kiln, or the glaze does not 'fit' the clay when it contracts on cooling, the glaze will craze – a series of fine lines will appear on the surface where the glaze has cracked. This is not a disaster, as the cracks are too fine to allow the pot to leak, but crazed surfaces are not as attractive as perfect ones. To avoid this when making earthenware make sure that the first firing is to a higher temperature (above 1100°C) than the second. An earthenware glaze melts between 950° and 1050°C. Stoneware glazes are slightly less susceptible to crazing and these melt between 1250° and 1300°C. They can be bought ready-made and must be put on cooking vessels. They can only be used, of course, if you have kiln facilities which reach these high temperatures.

Glazing technique

Factory-made pottery is glazed all over, the glazed surfaces being kept apart in the kiln by pointed triangles called 'stilts', and the triple marks of these are sometimes visible on the base of the finished pot. Beginners should not attempt to glaze pots all over but should leave the base unglazed. A shallow press-moulded bowl does not need glazing on the outside at all. A pot does not have to be glazed on both sides to be watertight and it is easier to handle both in the application of the glaze and in the firing if there are some unglazed surfaces.

There are many ways of applying glaze by dipping and pouring, and those which allow the potter somewhere dry to hold on to are the most successful. If fingers get in the way of the glaze they will cause an uneven thickness of application. I have seen people who are far from clumsy in everyday life become all fingers and thumbs when confronted with a glaze bucket and many good pots are spoiled at this glazing stage by indecisive handling. If you have a cylindrical shape to glaze, use a jug to fill up the inside of your pot with glaze, as shown in the diagram. Pour the glaze out again into the bucket as soon as it is full and an even coat will be

Glazing the inside of a pot.

left on the inside of your pot. Holding the pot by its base, press it head first into the glaze and immerse it to a point just short of your fingertips. An airlock will prevent glaze from flooding into the inside again, and when you raise the pot from the bucket give it a shake to clear any drops from the rim. If there are any droplets which will not shake off do not attempt to touch them while they are wet – let them dry completely and gently rub them down with a fingertip. Any other tool will pull the glaze away from the pot.

If you are glazing an open shape on the inside only, fill it with glaze and pour out as before, and clear away with a sponge any glaze which has run down the outside.

Open shapes to be glazed on both sides should be dipped in the glaze bucket, as shown in **the diagram, up to the half-way point** and then, when the first half has dried, picked up gently by the glazed surface and dipped in again so that the other half is covered. If the lines of glaze overlap there may be a slight change of colour after firing, but this is better than marks caused by fingers immersed with the pot in the glaze. If you make an untidy mess of glazing you can wash the glaze off entirely and start again, but you have to wait until the pot is completely dry before reapplying glaze, as a damp pot will not absorb enough water to leave an adequate coat.

Dip a cylindrical pot in the glaze up to your fingertips. Do not try to glaze its base.

The safest way to glaze an open shape.

88

Colours and decoration

Methods of applying decoration have already been described in Chapter 9, but a glaze is itself a form of decoration and many pots look their best if they are decorated all over with a plain coloured glaze.

A clear glaze must be used for a pot which has already been decorated with slip. Glaze colourants can be added to white or transparent glazes, though once the glaze has been mixed up, adding a fine ground colouring pigment and sieving can only be a chancy business if you do not know the dry weight of the glaze. Some colourants are stronger than others and rarely need to be more than ten per cent of the total weight in order to make the glaze go a strong colour. Ceramic catalogues list colourants by the names of metal oxides, though the colour you can expect is often **obvious from the name: cobalt oxide, for example, makes a strong** blue. It is difficult to produce reds and oranges, which is why pottery so coloured is rare and expensive. Many colours for mixing with glazes are offered in ceramic cataloques, where you will also find lists of 'underglaze' colours and sometimes 'on-glaze' colours. The beginner is often confused by these terms and can forget all about on-glaze colours, which are mostly used for the decoration at low temperatures of factory made 'blanks'. So-called underglaze colours are stains which can be either painted directly on to the biscuit pot or *after* the application of the glaze, before firing. Members of evening classes find that to use stains before the glaze application is anti-social, as some of the stain comes off in the glaze bucket and colours the glaze slightly for the next user.

Unfortunately the range of underglaze colours is so wide, with names like 'lilac' and 'salmon pink', that students are spoilt for choice. They would do better to stick to a couple of colours – red-brown produced by iron oxide and blue produced by cobalt oxide. These can be painted with a brush on to the glazed surface which will absorb moisture and dry the brush quickly. A technique of making simple marks without the dragging brush

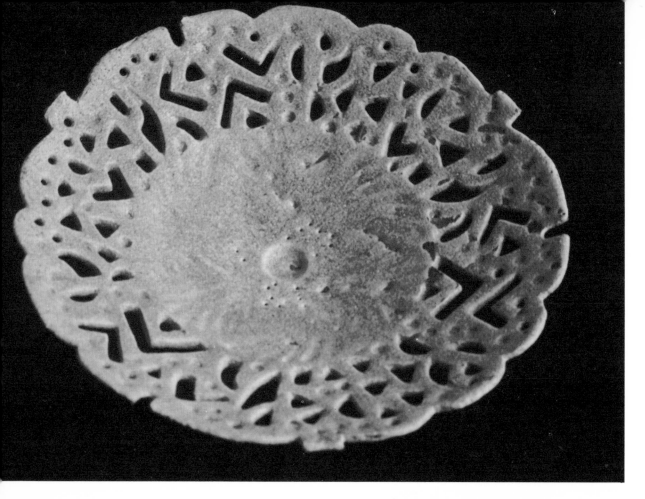

Left, above: *plain glaze on a bowl with perforated decoration by Ian Godfrey;* **below**: *design by Alan Wallwork created on a tile by melting into a clear glaze spots of colourant dropped on to the surface as the tile is slowly revolved.* **Above**: *three Roman drinking vessels,* c. AD 300, *ribbed by pressing the soft pot against a hard surface.*

movements associated with watercolour painting must therefore be learned. The same principles of design apply here as outlined in Chapter 9. Stop yourself from trying a detailed design on a small pot. Remember the value of repeating designs on round shapes and adapt your motif to curved surfaces. It is in the nature of glass to flow when molten and your painted design will flow with the glaze. The detailed designs on commercial china are often fired to low temperatures after the glaze has cooled and are not carried in the glaze. Your pot is going to gain both glaze and decoration in one operation, and you must expect your design to merge slightly into its surroundings. If you want to paint a design on your glaze, try to make a bold mark which will not be spoiled when it becomes blurred as part of the glass.

Tools

The glazing process is the last stage in the making of your pot. It can create a great deal of confusion if the working area is limited. Home potters should keep glaze in polythene buckets with lids, and will also need a fine rustless sieve or 'lawn', obtainable from ceramic suppliers, a plastic jug and a paintbrush. Convenient containers for colourants are yoghurt jars. Those who intend to add colourants to glazes really need a pestle and mortar to grind the material finely before adding to the glaze, but some people like the speckled effect which is the result of adding pigments without first grinding them. The production and perfection of glazes is the subject for a lifetime of research, and a great many detailed books are available on the subject. Those potters who want to experiment beyond the basic glazes already described are referred to the books listed on page 97.

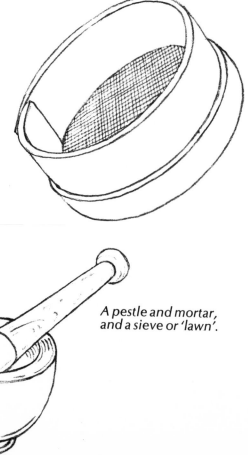

A pestle and mortar, and a sieve or 'lawn'.

Firing

Beginners at evening classes do not see much of the kiln or the firing process. Home potters who have bought their own kiln will have to pack it for themselves, and they must remember that pots must not touch either one another or the kiln wall, especially those pots which are glazed. The first, or biscuit, firing must be carried out slowly or the pots may break. Electric kilns have controls not unlike the domestic oven and a biscuit firing should be kept at *low* for two hours and *medium* for the next two, before turning on to *full*. A glaze firing can be started with the kiln on full and it must be watched very carefully when it is nearly at the required temperature. How do you know when this vital point is reached? If your kiln has a calibrated dial or pyrometer, you can read the temperature from this and switch off at the right time. Otherwise you have to put a small triangular pyramid inside the kiln when you are packing it in a position so that it will be visible through the spy hole. The kiln creates its own 'light' when it is hot, and you can watch the pyramid or 'Seger cone' bending over or 'squatting' as it reaches the temperature for which it is designed. It will change from a tall pyramid to a shape like a crooked finger. Cones are graded with numbers which correspond to fairly precise temperatures. A useful cone for an earthenware glaze is 'O3A', which represents 1060°C, and if three cones of ascending temperature are placed in the kiln together, as shown in the diagram, the watcher through the spy hole will have a very accurate knowledge of what is happening inside, as the cones squat in sequence. Cones are not easy to place in the kiln, and they are not easy to see at high temperatures when the glare from within the kiln is great, but they are accurate, while pyrometers can often be 50°C out. It is wise to use Seger cones in addition to a pyrometer as a double check when firing glazed pots, to avoid the disappointment of underfiring or the disaster of over-firing.

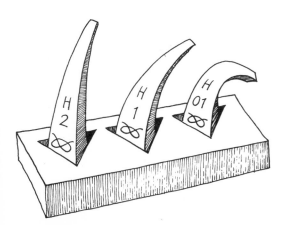

Seger cones after firing.

11   What is Good?

What is good? A surprising number of students lack confidence when they are making a pot, particularly if they are making it by hand and not on the wheel. They need a standard by which to judge their own work without imitating someone else's style or a tradition. They are reassured if their work is brought into close contact with other pottery and can stand up for itself. Good design, quality, finish, indeed perfection in pottery – all these are matters of opinion. A collector of fine porcelain might not look twice at a ginger beer jar, or even a Roman pot from a museum shelf. Similarly, a man who pays a high price for a broken, asymmetrical Persian bowl would not be impressed by tableware, even from celebrated manufacturers such as Wedgwood and Minton. A flower arranger might describe as a 'good shape' a vase that many of us would regard as hideous.

Only a ruthless admirer of technique can teach pottery enthusiastically without entering the area of aesthetics, and personal preferences are bound to show. A point that I must make is that even appropriateness of finish, surface, weight and detail, cannot be assessed in pottery by means of generalizations. It is all a question of the individual pot.

A pot does not have to be symmetrical to be good. It is not necessary to aim at lightness in the hand (or thinness of the clay); a rough and bubbly surface can be as thrilling as an even or unblemished one, and a brush or stencil design can be satisfying, if it is precise and intricate, or if it is ragged and abstract.

Pot by Hans Coper.

Pottery is an activity which can bring tremendous satisfaction. It can be pursued at leisure, alone or in company. It can and does take years to work through the many techniques which are mentioned in this book, and there are times when it is desperately disappointing or frustrating. It is always the pot which one most cares about which gets damaged in the kiln, broken or fails to live up to one's expectations when glazed. But, equally, the kiln can work its own magic and produce for you, from your own hands, a piece that appears to have all those qualities which make up a good pot: the right size and shape, colour and texture, and a tactile attraction that makes you want to hold it.

Beginners sometimes give up because of the difficulty of it all. They blame their own fingers for clumsiness before they have learnt the capabilities and responses of clay. They find the many methods of making and systems of decoration confusing. I hope that this book has helped to keep things straight, and has emphasized enough without being boring the importance of taking a simple idea and sticking to it, of giving a pot a suitable finish for its type. You are bound to learn by making mistakes, so when these mistakes happen, do not give up, build on them, and keep potting.

Further Reading

Billington, Dora, *The Technique of Pottery* London 1962

Birks, Tony, *The Potter's Companion* London and Glasgow 1974

Birks, Tony, *The Art of the Modern Potter* London 1967

Colbeck, John, *Pottery, the technique of throwing* London and New York, 1969

Leach, Bernard, *A Potter's Book* London 1940

Rhodes, Daniel, *Clay and Glazes for the Potter* Philadelphia, 1957

Rhodes, Daniel, *Kilns: Design, Construction and Operation* Philadelphia, 1968

Thorp, Harold E., *Basic Pottery for the Student* London, 1969

Picture Credits

Sources of Materials

In Britain

Clays

Moira Pottery Co. Ltd, Moira, Leicestershire

Morgan Refractories Ltd., Neston, Wirral, Cheshire

Potclays Ltd., Wharf House, Copeland Street, Hanley, Stoke on Trent, Staffs.

Materials

The Fulham Pottery Co. Ltd., 210 New Kings Road, London SW6 4NY

Podmore and Sons Ltd., Shelton, Stoke on Trent, Staffs.

Wengers Ltd., Etruria, Stoke on Trent, Staffs.

Wheels

Potters' Equipment Co., 17-18 Progress Way, Croydon, Surrey

J.W. Ratcliffe and Sons, Rope Street, Shelton New Road, Stoke on Trent, Staffs, ST4 6DJ

Kilns

Cromartie Kilns, Park Hill Road, Longton, Staffs.

Kilns and Furnaces Ltd., Keele Street, Tunstall, Stoke on Trent, Staffs.

Kasenit Ltd., Denbigh Road, Milton Keynes, MK1 1EQ, Bucks.

Kiln Plans

F.S. Dexter, Council for Small Industries in Rural Areas, 35 Camp Road, Wimbledon Common, London S.W.19.

In North America

Clays

Kentucky-Tennessee Clay Company, Mayfield, Ohio

Stewart Clay Company Inc., 133 Mulberry Street, New York, N.Y. 10013

United Clay Mines Corporation, 101 Oakland Street, Trenton, N.J.

Materials

Ferro Corporation, 4130 Easter 56th Street, Cleveland, Ohio

L.H. Butcher and Company, 3628 East Olympic Boulevard, San Francisco, California

Wheels

Gilmour Campbell, 14258 Maiden, Detroit, Michigan 48213

Scargo Pottery, Dennis, Cape Cod., Mass.

Kilns

Denver Fireclay Company, 3033 Black Street, Denver, Colorado

A.D. Alpine Inc., 353 Coral Circle, El Segundo, California 90245

Glossary and Index